SPANISH GALLEON
vs
ENGLISH GALLEON

1550–1605

MARK LARDAS

OSPREY PUBLISHING

Bloomsbury Publishing Plc

PO Box 883, Oxford, OX1 9PL, UK

1385 Broadway, 5th Floor, New York, NY 10018, USA

E-mail: info@ospreypublishing.com

www.ospreypublishing.com

OSPREY is a trademark of Osprey Publishing Ltd

First published in Great Britain in 2020

A catalogue record for this book is available from the British Library.

ISBN: PB 9781472839909; eBook 9781472839916; ePDF 9781472839886;
XML 9781472839893

20 21 22 23 24   10 9 8 7 6 5 4 3 2 1

Colour artwork illustrations: Adam Hook
Maps by Bounford.com
Index by Alison Worthington
Typeset by PDQ Digital Media Solutions, Bungay, UK
Printed and bound in India by Replika Press Private Ltd.

Author's acknowledgements

Thanks go to the Houston Maritime Museum and its dedicated staff,
especially Justin Parkoff. I would also like to thank William Wardle, a friend
from the Gulf Coast Ship Model Society, who generously let me use photos of
his models. I would also like to thank Kevin Crisman of the Institute of
Nautical Archaeology at Texas A&M University for his help in tracking down
several former graduate students, and Erika Elizabeth Laanela for help with
images. I also thank my son William, who has accompanied me on several
writing expeditions, serving as my photographer. He provided several of the
images in this book from some of our past excursions.

Dedication

This book is dedicated to Justin Parkoff, a scholar, a friend and a man who
knows galleons, real and imaginary. He has helped me on several book projects
because he is even more into marine archaeology than I am.

Editor's note

In most cases imperial measurements, including nautical miles (NM), knots
(kn) and long tons, have been used in this book. For ease of comparison please
refer to the following conversion table:

1 nautical mile (NM) = 1.85km
1 league = 3 NM
1 yard = 0.9m
1ft = 0.3m
1in. = 2.54cm/25.4mm
1kn = 1.85km/h
1 long ton = 1.02 metric tonnes
1 lb = 0.45kg

Front cover, above: The *Golden Hind* entering Callao Harbor (Lima, Peru)
with sails set and guns blazing, during Drake's circumnavigation of the world
(1577–80). On 15 February 1579, Drake arrived at Callao, causing panic. It
was here that he learnt of the recent departure of *Nuestra Señora de la
Concepción*, and set out in hot pursuit. (Adam Hook)
Front cover, below: The *Golden Hind* captures *Nuestra Señora de la Concepción*,
1 March 1579. (Adam Hook)

CONTENTS

INTRODUCTION

Sink me the ship, Master Gunner – sink her, split her in twain!
Fall into the hands of God, not into the hands of Spain!

(Tennyson, *The Revenge*)

The period 1550 to 1604 was crucial to the development of the modern world. Spain was at the height of its power, made rich by treasures of the New World. At the start of this period, England was a petty kingdom on the edge of Europe, but by its end, it was evolving into Great Britain, the global superpower that would dominate the world over the next two centuries. The key to both Spain and England's power lay in each nation's warships.

It was a period of contradiction, and remains one of the most romanticized periods of history for both Spain and Britain. For Spain, it represented the zenith of her power. For England, it was the start of her march to world domination.

During the 19th and 20th centuries, Spain looked back at this era with nostalgia. Conquistadores brought large amounts of the rest of the world under Spanish authority. Although small in number, they were seemingly invincible, with mere hundreds (or even dozens) bringing down vast empires in the name of God and Spain.

Nineteenth- and 20th-century Britain looked back at this period with pride. It was considered an era of plucky English Sea Dogs, fighting the odds against the formerly invincible Dons. England singed the beard of the King of Spain, and brought back wealth through doughty feats of arms.

In both cases, the romance was based on history. The world was expanding, seemingly exponentially, as trans-oceanic sea travel opened up new continents to European powers. The voyages, whether Portuguese, Spanish, English or French, were the stuff of adventure. Although filled with danger, if successful they could make a

poor man rich, and a rich man immensely wealthy. An example of the latter was Jakob Fugger, a German banker who lived between 1459 and 1521, and was said to have been the richest man in history, a wealth he derived from bankrolling Spanish exploration.

However, behind the romantic view of exploration lay a sordid reality. Travel by sea was a wretched experience, characterized by disease and squalor. Crowding and poor sanitary conditions made dysentery, typhoid fever and typhus rife. The food on board ships was awful and usually in short supply, and on more than one exploration voyage crews were reduced to eating their leatherwear and hunting shipboard rats for food. Scurvy was endemic. Storms and uncharted reefs tore ships apart. Yet apart from the hazards of the sea and the lack of fresh food, life at sea was only slightly less squalid than life ashore.

It was a violent age, more violent than the centuries that preceded the period 1550 to 1605. It was a time of religious turmoil, initiated by the Reformation, which started in 1517, and was then fanned into flames by the Counter-Reformation of 1530. By 1550, Europe was convulsed by religious wars that continued for 100 years. Catholics fought Protestants, Protestants fought Catholics, and different denominations of Protestantism fought each other in both civil and international wars. Spain, led by His Most Catholic Majesty, was on one side of the conflict, and England, led by a Protestant queen, was on the other.

It was not yet a time of political change. Except for a few of the more isolated societies – the Scandinavians with their Thing (a governing assembly), the Swiss with their cantons and Venice with its republic – representative government was non-existent. That change lay a century hence, in the period from 1642 through to 1792.

The modern conception of sea fights in the age of galleons: two ships exchanging broadsides until one sank. The reality was different. Boarding actions were more common than gunnery duels, and most battles were decided by boarding. (Author's collection)

This drawing is believed to depict *White Bear*, a galleon built in 1563, and rebuilt between 1585 and 1586 as a race-built galleon. The ship was rebuilt again in 1599, and served in the Royal Navy until 1627. Here it is shown after the 1585–86 rebuild. (Author's collection)

Monarchs did not reign, they ruled. Kings, princes and dukes ruled nations, frequently as absolute monarchs, occasionally advised by parliaments made up of the nobility. Queens, princesses and duchesses occasionally ruled, but they were exceptions, and were usually exceptional.

The period 1550 to 1605 was a time of immense change in naval architecture. Prior to 1480, virtually no ships crossed the world's oceans. The ships sailed by Christopher Columbus and Vasco da Gama on their voyages of exploration were designs optimized for short voyages along the European and Mediterranean coasts. Ships grew in size and rigs changed to accommodate trans-oceanic travel, as the wealth available from these new lands became apparent.

The immense wealth discovered in the New World and East Indies travelled to Europe by sea, largely in the bottoms of Spanish or Portuguese ships. Other nations were cut out of the game by the 1494 Treaty of Tordesillas, which divided lands outside Europe between Portugal and Spain along a line 370 leagues (1,110 NM) west of the Cape Verde Islands. After 1580, Spain forced Portugal into a dynastic union, merging the two countries. Virtually all of the wealth went directly to Spain.

It also meant the ships carrying this treasure – be it silver, dyewood (providing dye for textiles) or cochineal (to make carmine) from the Americas, or spices and silks from the Far East – were valuable and tempting targets, especially for England and France. These nations on Europe's Atlantic coast, barred by Spain from exploiting this wealth through commerce, chose to seize it through piracy. This meant they also required ships.

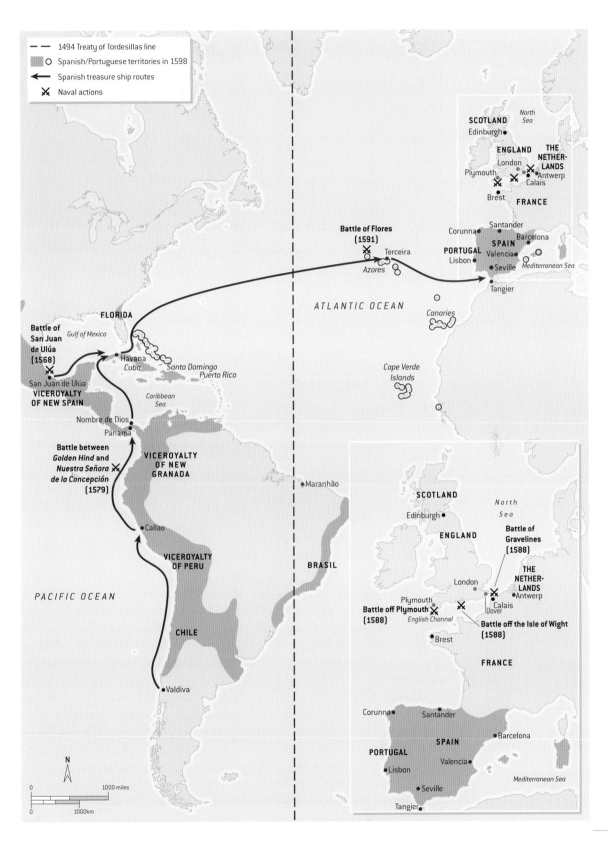

1494 Treaty of Tordesillas line

Spanish/Portuguese territories in 1598

Spanish treasure ship routes

Naval actions

SCOTLAND
North Sea
Edinburgh•

ENGLAND
London•
Plymouth•
Brest•

THE NETHER-LANDS
•Antwerp
Calais

FRANCE

Battle of Flores (1591)
Terceira
Azores

Corunna•
Santander•
•Barcelona
SPAIN
Valencia•
PORTUGAL
Lisbon•
•Seville
Mediterranean Sea

ATLANTIC OCEAN

Canaries

Tangier•

FLORIDA
Gulf of Mexico

Battle of San Juan de Ulúa (1568)
•Havana
Cuba
San Juan de Ulúa•
VICEROYALTY OF NEW SPAIN

Santa Domingo
Puerto Rico

Caribbean Sea

Cape Verde Islands

Nombre de Dios•
Panama•

Battle between *Golden Hind* and *Nuestra Señora de la Concepción* (1579)

VICEROYALTY OF NEW GRANADA

•Maranhão

•Callao

PACIFIC OCEAN

VICEROYALTY OF PERU

BRASIL

CHILE

•Valdiva

SCOTLAND
Edinburgh•

ENGLAND

North Sea

Battle of Gravelines (1588)

London•

THE NETHER-LANDS
•Antwerp
Calais
Dover

Plymouth•
Battle off Plymouth (1588)
English Channel

Battle off the Isle of Wight (1588)

•Brest

FRANCE

Corunna•
Santander•
•Barcelona
SPAIN
Valencia•
PORTUGAL
•Lisbon
•Seville
Mediterranean Sea
Tangier•

N

0   1000 miles
0   1000km

A 16th-century galleon under cruising sails. With its high structure, it is probably Spanish, or built by a Mediterranean nation, such as Venice or Genoa. It is sailing under topsails and fore course, under a following wind. (Author's collection)

By the middle of the 16th century, a new class of warship emerged in response to the need for armed oceanic ships. It was called the galleon. It was not only designed to operate on long trans-oceanic voyages, but was also designed to carry a broadside of heavy artillery. It was the capital ship of the age, and although smaller than the great ships (like the *Mary Rose*) that preceded it, it was more seaworthy, more manoeuvrable and faster.

The galleon became the symbol of the age for both Spain and England, although relatively few of the ships on the oceans were of this type. Carracks, naos, hulks and caravels populated the oceans. Yet the galleon fired imaginations. Battles were fought between galleons, and many of these remain well known today. While true duels between galleons rarely happened, those that did still evoke great interest.

This book tells their stories: what it took to build a galleon, to sail a galleon and to fight a galleon. It also explores the reality behind the romance of these ships and their famous captains.

CHRONOLOGY

1492
12 October   Christopher Columbus, sailing for Spain, lands in the Bahamas, opening the Americas to European exploration, conquest and settlement.

1497
24 June   John Cabot, sailing under the English flag, discovers Newfoundland, staking an English claim in the New World.

1532
John Hawkins is born in Plymouth, England.
Pedro Sarmiento de Gamboa is born.

1540
Francis Drake is born in a cottage near Tavistock, Devon.

1542
June   Richard Grenville is born.

1554
25 July   Philip, heir to the Spanish throne, marries Queen Mary I of England.

1556
21 May   Upon the abdication of his father, Charles V, Philip becomes Philip II, ruler of Spain, Naples and Sicily, Milan and the Netherlands.

1558
17 November   Upon the death of Queen Mary, Elizabeth Tudor becomes Queen Elizabeth I of England.

1562
John Hawkins begins his first voyage to Africa and the Americas.

Anchors recovered from the *San Esteban*, which wrecked off South Padre Island, in the Gulf of Mexico, in 1554. The anchors were recovered when *San Esteban* was excavated between 1973 and 1975. They are on display at Corpus Christi Museum of Science and History, Texas. The wooden stocks are modern reconstructions. (Author's collection)

1564

John Hawkins begins his second voyage to Africa and the Americas. Francis Drake joins the expedition, commanding a ship.

1566

Francis Drake gains his first command, the merchant vessel *Judith*.

1567

Philip II sends an army into the Netherlands to enforce Catholic worship.
John Hawkins, with Drake commanding *Judith*, begins his third slave-trading voyage to Africa and the Americas.

1568
24 September — Spanish ships attack English ships at San Juan de Ulúa, destroying or capturing three of the five ships of John Hawkins' third trading expedition to Spanish possessions in the New World.

1568

The largely Protestant northern provinces of the Netherlands rebel against Spanish rule.

1570

Drake conducts his first voyage to reconnoitre the West Indies. His second voyage follows in 1571.

1572
24 May — Drake sets sail from Plymouth with the ships *Pascha* and *Swan* to raid the Isthmus of Panama – his first raiding voyage.

1577
26 November — John Hawkins is appointed Treasurer of the Royal Navy, a position he holds until 1595.

1577

Elizabeth begins subsidizing the Dutch Protestant rebels led by William the Silent.
Revenge and *Golden Hind* are launched.
17 December — Drake sails with five ships from Plymouth to raid the Pacific coast of Spanish America.

1578

Philip II appoints Alexander Farnese, Duke of Parma, as Governor-General of the Netherlands.
1 November — Drake enters the Pacific with one ship, *Golden Hind*.

1579
7 February — Drake sacks the port of Callao (Lima, Peru).
27 February — Sarmiento, with two ships, sets off from Callao in pursuit of Drake, but fails to locate him.
1 March — *Golden Hind* captures *Nuestra Señora de la Concepción* during a fight near Esmeraldas, Ecuador.

1580
24 July — King Henry of Portugal dies. Don Antonio de Crato declares himself King of Portugal.
19 August — Sarmiento arrives in Spain after failing to find Drake, passing the Straits of Magellan west to east.
26 September — Drake, with *Golden Hind*, arrives at Plymouth with treasure valued between £337,000 and £1.5 million.

1581
13 April — Philip II of Spain is crowned King of Portugal.

1582
25–26 July — Álvaro de Bazán, 1st Marquis of Santa Cruz, defeats the naval forces of Don Antonio de Crato at the Battle of Ponta Delgada, securing the Azores for King Philip of Spain.

1584

11 August — Sarmiento is captured by English privateers.

1585

September–July — Drake leads an expedition of 21 ships to raid Spain, the Cape Verde Islands, Santo Domingo (Dominican Republic) and the South American coast.

1586

August — Queen Elizabeth I releases Sarmiento, giving him a peace proposal to carry to King Philip II.

1587

Following the execution of Mary, Queen of Scots, Philip II decides to invade England and replace Elizabeth with a Catholic queen. He appoints the Marquis of Santa Cruz to command the invasion fleet.

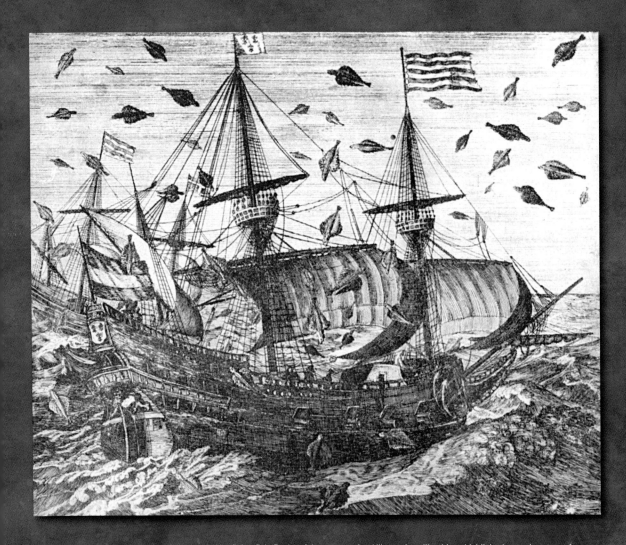

An English galleon in tropical waters, surrounded by flying fish. Books of the era contained illustrations like this to highlight the exotic nature of Caribbean waters. (Author's collection)

12 April–6 July Drake leads an expedition of four royal galleons, 20 privateer galleons and pinnaces to destroy the impending Spanish Armada in port. It destroys the Spanish ships in Cadiz, attacks Lisbon and captures a Portuguese treasure ship, delaying the invasion of England by a year.

1588
9 February The Marquis of Santa Cruz dies. Alonso Pérez de Guzmán, 7th Duke of Medina Sidonia, is appointed as the replacement commander of the *Empresa de Inglaterra* (Enterprise of England).

19 July The Spanish Armada arrives in the English Channel.

21 July The Armada attempts to seize Plymouth, but fails.

25 July The Armada attempts a landing on the Isle of Wight, but is driven off.

28 July The Armada anchors off Calais.

29 July The Battle of Gravelines; the Armada is scattered, and the *San Mateo* is captured by Dutch rebels.

1589
Philip II orders 12 new galleons built in 'English' fashion. These become known as the 'Twelve Apostles'.

19 April The English Counter-Armada sails to destroy the Spanish fleet in port and establish Don Antonio on the Portuguese throne. It fails abjectly.

1591
5 April A 29-ship fleet departs Plymouth under the command of Lord Thomas Howard to capture the year's Spanish treasure fleet as it approaches the Azores.

4 August A 59-ship Spanish fleet under the command of Alonso de Bazán (Marquis del Viso, and brother of Álvaro de Bazán) departs Ferrol, Spain to intercept the English ships off the Azores.

30–31 August The Battle of Flores. *Revenge* fights the Spanish fleet, engaging five ships and sinking two.

10 September Richard Grenville dies of wounds suffered during the Battle of Flores.

1595
12 November John Hawkins dies at sea off Portobelo during Drake's final expedition.

1596
28 January Francis Drake dies off the coast of Portobelo, Panama during a buccaneering expedition to the Spanish Main (its colonies in the Americas).

1598
13 September King Philip II dies, aged 71.

1603
March Queen Elizabeth I of England dies, aged 69.

1604
28 August The Treaty of London is signed, ending the war between Spain and England.

1608
Pedro Sarmiento de Gamboa dies, probably in Manila.

DESIGN AND DEVELOPMENT

One problematic area of a study about galleon duels is that virtually every famous sea battle between two ships in the period 1550–1600 is described as a fight between two galleons, even when the ships involved were great ships, carracks, caravels or naos, or some mixture of the types. To many, any armed 16th-century ship with square sails on the main and lateen sails on the after masts, towering forecastles and stern castles, must be a galleon. This type of confusion is common. The best-known recent example is the fight between the *Bonhomme Richard* and *Serapis*, where both ships (two-deckers) are commonly referred to as frigates (a different warship entirely).

The period between 1550 and 1605 saw revolutionary growth in naval architecture. The changes are not apparent to modern readers, but in many ways they were as significant as the changes seen in warships between 1850 and 1905. The galleon emerged a little before that period, and matured into the most prominent fighting ship of the era, a specific and identifiable type.

THE GALLEON

The galleon can be defined as a warship, with multiple decks and three or four masts, that was designed to carry a battery of 18–24 heavy cannon on its lower gun deck. It carried square sails on its fore- and mainmasts, and a lateen sail on its mizzenmast and its fourth mast (called the bonaventure mast), if it had one. The name most likely

Developed in the 1400s as an ocean-going, cargo-carrying ship, the carrack formed the basis for the galleon. This model shows a typical carrack with high forecastle and sterncastle, and a prominent beakhead. It is not built around a gun deck. (Author's collection)

came from the Portuguese *galeão* (or warship). Its distinguishing visible feature was a prominent and built-up beakhead, forward of the hull of the ship. Galleons had built up fore- and sterncastles, although these were typically lower than the towering forecastles of the great ships of the late 15th century and first half of the 16th century.

Galleons were ocean-going ships, but not necessarily large vessels. They displaced between 300 and 1,500 tons, and were typically 100–150ft long on their gun deck. (By comparison, a full-rigged 18th-century, 20-gun sloop-of-war displaced 300–450 tons, while a 74-gun ship-of-the-line of that period displaced 1,500–2,000 tons.) The median displacement of English galleons was around 500 tons. Spanish galleons averaged slightly larger displacements.

Most galleons were built by syndicates of private investors for use as cargo carriers, rather than by countries for their national navies. National navies of the era were small. Common practice during wartime was to impress merchant vessels for naval service. A galleon, with its sturdy construction, capacious hold and potentially large gun battery could serve commercial shippers in several roles: as a privateer, as a ship to transport valuable cargoes (on government charters during peacetime) or under lease to the crown as a warship during times of war. If a galleon was drafted by the government during wartime, it was more likely to survive and be returned to its owner than a weaker vessel.

The galleon was an outgrowth of a ship called a carrack or nao. The carrack also had three or four masts, and was the first ship to be truly capable of crossing oceans:

stable in stormy seas and capable of carrying stores for a multi-month voyage. Such vessels made most of the voyages to the New World or the East Indies that took place in the first half of the 16th century. They had a high, rounded stern, and a large forecastle and sterncastle. The *Santa Maria*, a nao, could be called a carrack. *Victoria*, the flagship of Portuguese explorer Ferdinand Magellan, was a carrack.

The galleon borrowed the carrack's basic hull form, although the former tended to have a higher length-to-beam ratio than the carrack. A carrack's hull was not fine, however. Length-to-beam ratios tended to range from 3:1 to 3.3:1. (By contrast, the length-to-beam ratio of USS *Constitution* was 4:1, and that of 19th-century clippers ranged from 5:1 to 6:1.) Less portly than carracks (which sometimes had length-to-beam ratios of 2.5:1), galleons were swifter than the carracks or great ships.

In the Middle Ages, many ships were shell-built: the keel was installed, and then the planking was added around the keel until the hull form emerged, with the planks overlapping (called clinker-built planking). Only after the hull had been planked were the ship's frames installed, carved to fit the curve of the hull. This method is still used today to build small wooden boats. While satisfactory for creating ships of the sizes desired in the 1200s through to the 1400s, the size and strength of hulls built in this manner were both limited.

Carracks and galleons were frame-built and carvel planked (i.e. with hull planks laid edge to edge and attached to the frame). In a frame-built ship, the frames defining the hull's form were added after the keel was built. Only then was the hull planked. Rather than overlapping, the planks were laid end to end, creating a smooth hull. Frame-built ships had a stronger structure, allowing larger and more robust ships to be built.

A model of an early Spanish galleon, created by Bill Wardell. It illustrates the high superstructure typical of Spanish galleons built prior to the 1550s. (Author's collection)

GREAT GUNS

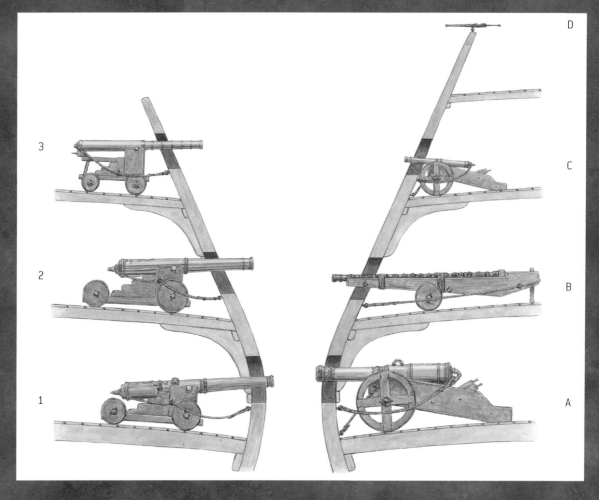

A galleon's effectiveness lay in its battery of guns. This plate shows the range of artillery carried by English and Spanish galleons.

To the left is a race-built English galleon displaying its typical broadside guns. All are mounted on four-wheel truck carriages:

1. Culverin (gun deck): A long-range, ship-killing, brass muzzleloader. Culverins fired an 18 lb shot.

2. Demi-culverin (upper deck): Another long-range, brass muzzleloader, firing an 8 lb ball.

3. Minion: A lighter gun that fired a 5¼ lb ball capable of penetrating the bulwarks of the upper deck and the castles.

To the right is the larger and loftier Spanish galleon mounting guns on four decks. Spanish muzzleloaders of the 16th century were typically mounted on two-wheel field carriages, while breechloaders were on sledge carriages, frequently with two wheels allowing repositioning:

A. Demi-cannon (gun deck): A brass muzzleloader that threw a 32 lb shot. The range of the demi-cannon was shorter than a culverin due to the demi-cannon barrel's shorter length. The ball also had a slower muzzle velocity.

B. Iron breechloading bombard (upper deck): Obsolescent by the time of the Armada campaign, Spain still used them due to shortages of newer brass breechloaders. It typically fired stone shot.

C. Saker: A short-range, brass muzzleloader, firing a 6 lb ball. Probably cast in England, it was smuggled to Spain.

D. Verso: A breechloading iron gun on a swivel mount set in the bulwark. Man-killing pieces, versos fired 4 oz. to 1 lb of solid lead, stone or iron shot, occasionally scrap iron.

Frame-building was also a more complicated method of shipbuilding. In shell construction, the hull form was defined by the planking. In frame construction, the frames had to be planned before the ship was built, and built to closer tolerances, to assure a hull form that was 'fair' – without humps or hollows along the waterline due to a frame being too wide or too narrow compared to its adjacent frames for the correct waterline. This complication was worth tolerating for the gains in size and strength that frame-building offered.

What defined a galleon was its gun deck, even if it had been built by private investors or was often used as merchant vessels. Carracks carried guns, but most were on the weather decks, as opposed to the lower decks (or gun decks). While not the first class of warship to carry a broadside of guns, the galleon was the first class of warship designed and built to carry a broadside of ship-killing guns – ones heavy enough to severely damage hull structure.

A model of *Pelican*, later renamed *Golden Hind*, a typical small English galleon. While not a race-built ship, with a low-slung forecastle, it was definitely more seaworthy than the Spanish galleon previously pictured, with a less prominent superstructure. (Author's collection)

Earlier warships such as *Mary Rose* or *Henry Grace à Dieu* (*Great Harry*) were a class known as great ships. They were specifically built as warships, but the cannon were an afterthought, added after the ship was built, located on decks positioned by tradition rather than to carry cannon. Initially, little thought was given to the effect of the cannon on the ship's stability or seaworthiness. In many cases, their lower gunports would be at or slightly below the waterline on a ship's leeward (downwind) side when the ship heeled (tilted) in the wind. When sailing in a stiff wind, these gunports would be sealed and caulked (made watertight), with only the ports on the windward or upwind side open.

Before a ship changed tack (the act of turning into the wind so the sail moves to the opposite side), the windward gunports had to be closed and sealed. If the wind changed unexpectedly, and windward became leeward, those open gunports would suddenly find themselves below the waterline, allowing water to rush in and sink the ship. This happened to *Mary Rose*. Alternatively, sometimes the guns were placed so that when the ship heeled beyond a certain angle, it would continue heeling until it capsized. (Naval architects were still working on perfecting stability in 1628, when the Swedish warship *Vasa* capsized due to a lack of stability.)

The galleon was the first attempt at solving these problems. The gun deck was placed at what was thought to be the best location for the guns in terms of stability and seaworthiness. The lower gun deck was raised to keep the gunports above the

A model of *Henry Grace à Dieu* (also known as *Great Harry*). A multi-deck warship, it was built on the principles of the carrack. Note how close the lowest gun deck is to the waterline. These gunports would have to be shut and sealed on the lee side, lest water rush in and sink the ship, as happened to *Mary Rose*. (Author's collection)

water, but kept low enough so that the guns' weight would not compromise stability. They were built with a sheer forward (the sheer is a measure of longitudinal main deck curvature). Often, the after two broadside guns were placed on a platform lower than the lower gun deck to prevent them from being mounted too high above the sea.

Although some galleons had two gun decks, the second gun deck always carried lighter guns. This was necessary lest the ship capsize if hit by a stiff gust. There was almost always one row of heavy guns. The only exceptions were prestige ships, used mainly to display status, and which rarely ventured far from port.

A galleon had two or three decks (running the length of the ship) and several platforms (i.e. partial decks, extending only over a portion of the hull). At the bottom of the hull was the hold. It was used for storage, and was capacious enough to carry provisions for six months and still have room for cargo. Since many of the cargoes coming to Europe were low-volume, high-value goods (gold, silver, cochineal, spices, china and silk), well-armed galleons were perfect ships in which to move these goods.

Above the hull was a series of platforms, known collectively as the orlop. These would include platforms for the cable tier (where the anchor cables were stored) and storerooms forward, and the bread room and magazine aft. There was also often a platform aft for the after two broadside guns. These could be shifted to serve as stern chasers (i.e. aiming rearwards).

Above the orlop was the gun deck. The port and starboard guns were sometimes staggered rather than aligned (as they would be from the 17th century onward). These cannon were longer than later designs. The breech might go beyond the centreline when run in.

Except for the very largest galleons, which sometimes had an upper gun deck, the next deck up would be the upper deck. This was a weather deck, with portions exposed to the elements, especially in the centre (or waist). This deck also had gunports and carried guns, but these guns would be much lighter than those on the gun deck. They were better used as man killers than ship killers.

Above the structural portion of the hull, a galleon had three superstructures: a beakhead, a forecastle and a sterncastle. The castles were what the name implied: a series of platforms at the ship's front (forecastle) and rear (sterncastle) intended as a place for men to fight from and for offering rudimentary protection from enemy fire.

Stone and iron cannonballs of the 16th century. These were recovered from the *San Esteban*, which sank in 1554. They are typical of the ammunition used by England and Spain. (William Lardas)

These emerged in pre-gunpowder times to give archers a platform from which to fight – the higher the better. On great ships, these towered three to four layers high. Galleons typically had one or two levels for the forecastle, and two or possibly three in the sterncastle. The sides were planked in for protection, and guns were mounted in all levels of the castles, although these were typically light guns, often swivels at the highest levels.

The beakhead was a platform projecting forward of the hull. It was generally located halfway between the gun deck and the upper deck, and was usually accessible through both. It was used to position archers and arquebusmen, as a stage to assemble boarders during battle, and as a platform for the men handling the spritsail (the square sail mounted on the bowsprit). Beakheads were also the location of the 'seat-of-ease', the crew's latrine. Beakheads of the era were prominent and sturdy. They sometimes ran half the length of the bowsprit.

Galleons were armed with two types of cannon: breechloading cannon made of built-up iron, and cast bronze muzzleloaders. While iron breechloaders were still common in 1550, by 1605 they were almost entirely replaced by cast muzzleloaders.

The breechloading cannon was the oldest type of naval artillery. Developed in the late 14th century, these guns were made in the manner of a cooper making a barrel. A collection of wrought iron bars was fitted together in a cylinder and roughly welded together. Iron hoops were then sweated onto the cylinder at short intervals. An alternative method was to take a series of short iron cylinders, with the ends tapered to fit into each other. Iron hoops were then placed to cover the joints, and heated on.

The resulting tube was open at both ends, and was fixed into a wooden cradle. A second, shorter chamber was made with an iron plug at the end; this contained the gunpowder charge. The ball was placed in the barrel, the chamber with the gunpowder

A model of a very early three-masted ship. The hull appears to be that of a cog or a hulk. The mainsail would blanket the foresail with a following wind, but fore and mizzen made the ship easier to turn. This is an early 15th-century ship. (Author's collection)

charge was fitted in behind the ball, and a block of wood was hammered in between the rear of the chamber and the back of the gun carriage, in order to seal the chamber to the barrel and minimize gas leakage when the gun was fired.

It was a makeshift, weak form of artillery, which could not throw a ball very hard or very fast. When overcharged with gunpowder, it could explode. But until metalworkers developed forges hot enough to pour molten iron into a mould, it was the only way to make a cannon. Known as lombards and bombards, these cannon were the main shipboard artillery through the early 16th century.

By the end of the 15th century, technology had advanced to a point where smoothbore muzzleloading cannon could be cast from bronze, and by the middle of the 16th century, English gunfounders had learned how to cast artillery in iron (iron muzzleloaders began appearing on ships in the early 1600s). *Mary Rose* had around 30 cast bronze cannon by 1530, and by the 1560s, cast bronze English cannon were in demand for both English and Spanish ships. The Spanish purchased theirs through smugglers, and could never acquire enough.

These guns were much larger than the built-up wrought iron breechloaders, and quickly supplanted them. However, the wrought iron breechloaders continued in use through much of the 16th century. There were never enough cannon to equip the constantly growing European fleets, and it was not until near the end of the century that the supply of cast ordinance increased sufficiently to retire the remaining breechloaders.

MANOEUVRING A GALLEON

A galleon could not steer directly into the wind. If it needed to cross the wind direction to change course, it could either tack (turn into the wind, as shown in **A**) or wear (turn away from the wind until it was on its new course, as shown in **B**). Wearing was safer, but it took longer and cost ground, as you had to start by going in the direction you had come from. Tacking was faster, but difficult (the process is shown in this illustration; wind direction is indicated by the arrows).

1. A ship starts close-hauled, as close to the wind as it can sail with the sails still drawing.

2. The helm is thrown over to turn the ship into the wind. As it turns, the foremast sails and spritsail are back to push the bow in the direction of the turn, while the mizzen and bonaventure sails push the stern in the opposite direction.

3. The mainsail and lateen sails are set parallel to the wind, while the foremast sails and spritsail continue backed, pushing the bow away from the wind on the new tack.

4. All the sails are placed filling on the new tack, close-hauled on the opposite tack from which the ship started.

The sail structure of galleons was the result of 200 years of evolution. As late as the 14th century, two types of rigs were common on all ships: a single-mast vessel with a single square sail, and a two-mast ship with two lateen sails. The former was most common in northern Europe, the latter most common in the Mediterranean.

The cog (or Kogge) was the supreme example of the northern, single-mast, square-sail merchantman. It appeared in the late 10th century, and became the queen of the northern seas during the 14th century. It was replaced briefly by the hulk, another single-mast design with a larger and double-ended hull, during the next hundred years. The hulk shared many of the cog's limitations. The single mast limited the manoeuvrability of the ship, and there was a limit to the size of a ship with a single square sail. If a ship displaced much more than 100 tons, it was difficult to get a sail large enough to move the ship at an economical speed.

In the Mediterranean, the lateen sail dominated. This was a triangular sail with the forward edge attached to a long spar running diagonally on a short mast. It had several advantages in the confined waters of the Mediterranean, where much of the traffic followed coastlines or confined channels between islands. It allowed a ship to sail closer to the wind; it required a smaller crew to handle; and the short mast made it easier to outfit. Tall, straight pines for masts, common along the Baltic and North Sea coasts, were harder to source.

John Hawkins was a merchant adventurer in the 1560s. He became treasurer of the navy in 1577, and used his seagoing experience to develop the highly effective race-built galleon. (Author's collection)

Additionally, two lateen masts made a ship easier to handle. Mariners could use the leverage of the sails to assist the rudder in turning the ship. It was for this reason that the caravel, developed by Portugal for exploring the African coast, was typically outfitted with two lateen masts. It allowed the ship the manoeuvrability needed to keep off a lee shore. The lateen rig's only real disadvantage was that it was inefficient in a following wind – yet a following wind was what northern European (and later trans-oceanic) ships typically encountered.

At some point early in the 15th century, perhaps as early as 1410, a northern shipowner realized that a lateen mast aft of the mainmast could solve some of the steering problems inherent in a single-mast rig. A few northern ships began adding a small mast (soon renamed the mizzenmast) aft of the great mast on which the main sail was set. Within 20 years, the mizzenmast with a lateen sail became common, and the great mast was now the mainmast.

The next addition was a mast ahead of the mainmast. The second mast allowed a second square sail to be set. Not only was the sail area

NUESTRA SEÑORA DE LA CONCEPCIÓN

Estimated dimensions[1]

Tons burthen:	120 tons
Length of deck:	90ft
Beam:	23ft
Draft:	9ft
Crew:	Between 60 and 100 men

[1] These dimensions are estimates and approximations. No measurements were made during its lifetime, and all depictions of its appearance are conjectural.

Nuestra Señora de la Concepción (*Our Lady of the Immaculate Conception*) was a Spanish galleon that sailed in the Pacific during the last half of the 16th century and the first half of the 17th. It was nicknamed *Cacafuego* ('shit-fire') because it was the most heavily armed Spanish ship in the Pacific in 1578. Its place of construction and launch date are unknown, but it probably had been in the Pacific only a few years and was a relatively new ship when Drake captured it on 1 March 1578. It may have been built in Acapulco or Callao. Drake released the ship after offloading its cargo to *Golden Hind*, rewarding the crew and passengers with some of the loot taken by the English.

It continued carrying treasure along the Pacific coast of North and Central America for many years, and served as the Manila–Acapulco galleon (carrying silver to China, and spices, porcelain, ivory, lacquerware and silk cloth back to Mexico) several times. It was reported lost in a typhoon in 1638, wrecked on Saipan, while returning from Manila with a load of spices, ivory, jade and camphor. It is possible this ship may have been a later ship named *Nuestra Señora de la Concepción*, as the ship captured by Drake would have been over 60 years old by 1638.

increased, but the ship's manoeuvrability increased, especially if the mainmast were stepped at the ship's centre of mass – the ship's pivot point. The combination of the foresail and the mizzen increased the leverage in turning the ship.

However, the second mast added complications to sailing a ship. With a cog or other similarly rigged ship, the best point of sailing was with a soldier's wind – the wind dead astern, which blanketed sails on a multi-mast ship. With a second mast, the best point of sail was with the wind from astern, but at an angle. This angle varied from ship to ship. It could be anywhere from 15

A model of a large Spanish galleon. This is a late-period ship, built after 1588, possibly one of the Twelve Apostles. While retaining a high forecastle, the sterncastle is significantly lower than that of the Spanish galleon pictured on page 15. (Houston Maritime Museum; author's photograph)

degrees to 45 degrees off the stern. But the three-mast configuration – with square sails on the forward two masts and a lateen mizzen aft – had so many advantages that it dominated other configurations. It was almost universal on galleons.

The only exception was the addition of a fourth mast aft of the mizzen. This bonaventure mast was added to overcome the inertia created by the tall superstructure of a galleon. This exposed area acted as a fixed sail, one that could not be trimmed, and which resisted attempts to turn the ship, especially in strong winds. The bonaventure mizzen increased the length of the moment arm from the extra after mast to the mainmast, increasing the turning leverage on a ship.

While the galleon's hull form and rig was crude compared to the full-rigged ship at the heyday of the age of sail in the early 19th century, the galleon was a substantial improvement over earlier designs. It could go faster, carry more and hit harder than any other class of ship in the 16th century. Like the frigate and 74-gun two-decker in the 18th century, it combined the various elements that went into building a ship in a way that made it legendary. In many ways, it was the first modern sailing ship.

SPANISH CONSTRUCTION

Originally an Italian design, the galleon was adopted by Portugal and quickly copied by Spain, appearing in those countries between 1517 and 1530. Much of the original design of Spanish galleons was defined by two Spanish captain-generals, Pedro Menéndez de Avilés and Álvaro de Bazán. They adapted the carrack design, lowered the superstructure, increased the length-to-breadth ratio and added a gun deck. These, along with the Portuguese galleons, were intended to escort convoys, protecting the lightly armed carracks from marauding pirates. By 1550, galleons were widely used by the Spanish and Portuguese navies.

Spain preferred large galleons. Spanish galleons also tended to be taller than those of other nations. Part of this was due to Spain's sea fighting tactics. For a much longer period than northern European nations (especially England), Spain viewed naval combat as an extension of land warfare. Fought as a series of boarding actions, it culminated in the soldiers boarding and taking an enemy ship as if they were storming a castle. The galleon's artillery served to soften up the enemy's resistance before the inevitable boarding action. This attitude continued even after wrought iron guns were replaced with larger cast cannon.

A larger ship provided several advantages in a mêlée battle. It could carry a larger contingent of soldiers, which improved their odds of outnumbering the forces resisting boarding. Once the single-shot firearms and crossbows had been discharged, there was no time to reload. The battle became hand-to-hand, and cold steel decided the action. The side with the most blades in action generally won.

Larger ships also tended to be taller than smaller ships. In a mêlée, this provided the equivalent of the high ground. The bigger galleon's soldiers could attack downhill, while any attempt to board the bigger galleon was literally an uphill fight.

While the bigger galleon was less manoeuvrable and slower than a smaller galleon, it was faster than most other types of vessels, especially carracks, the most common merchant ship. Assuming the battle would be decided in a boarding action, being slow and ungainly seemed less of a disadvantage to the Spanish. The enemy ships could flee, but they could not defeat you if they ran. All they could do was delay the inevitable boarding action. If they escaped today, there would be another chance tomorrow.

To an extent, Spain cut its coat to meet the cloth available when it came to galleon design. Spain had plenty of soldiers available to man ships when necessary, but had difficulty finding guns. Due to the inadequacy of her gunfounding industry, Spain was dependent upon imports for enough cannon to equip all her galleons. As the century progressed, many of the best countries from which to buy artillery – Sweden and England, for example – were Protestant. These heretic nations, which Spain wished to subdue, had no interest in selling Spain the rope with which she would hang them. Building galleons designed to optimize the shortage of artillery and ready supply of men meant building larger galleons.

ENGLISH CONSTRUCTION

England had begun building galleons by 1545, when *Anne Gallant* and *Grand Mistress* appeared on the rolls of Henry VIII's fleet. Described as sister ships, displacing 450 tons, they had the galleon's requisite two decks (including a gun deck) with built-up castles. Built in England, the design borrowed heavily from Venetian examples. Two 300-ton, French-designed galleons, *Salamander* and *Unicorn*, were captured from the Scots in 1544. These four ships, all admired for their sailing characteristics, were the first English galleons, and formed the basis of English galleon construction.

Few galleons were added to the English navy during the rest of Henry VIII's reign through to the end of Mary I's rule in 1558. Henry built a fleet centred on great ships between 1515 and 1545. By the time these ships had aged, Mary I was married to Philip II of Spain. She had little incentive to expand the English navy. In the early years of Elizabeth I's reign, financial constraints prevented her from expanding the navy.

Galleons were not only built for the crown: they were ordered by commercial syndicates, such as the Muscovy Company. These trading companies needed cargo ships capable of providing their own defence on long voyages. By the mid-1570s, English shipyards were cranking out galleons, built for both the crown and for gentlemen adventurers seeking fortunes through trade or privateering.

These English galleons tended to be smaller than Spanish ships. *Golden Hind* displaced only 300 tons, yet was a galleon, while many others only displaced 300–500 tons. This was a handy size for a commercial syndicate: the lower cost for building the smaller ship reduced the syndicate's exposure if the galleon were lost, and more shipyards could build the smaller ships. Finding enough cargo to fill a 1,000-ton galleon, at least in the 1560s to 1580s, was, for the English, a challenge.

Yet the main reason for the smaller size was the English emphasis on speed and handling in their galleons. Galleons displacing 400–500 tons generally went faster than the larger Spanish galleons, and outmanoeuvred them.

When John Hawkins became Treasurer of the Royal Navy in 1578, he used his past naval combat experience to improve galleon design. Hawkins ordered the race-built galleon, with lower forecastle and sterncastle than earlier galleons, a higher length-to-beam ratio and a lower hull. These ships could choose the distance at which they fought an enemy: they could stand off and bombard a larger foe until it suffered sufficient damage to allow it to be boarded, or they could swoop in to take a merchantman carrack before its escorts could interfere. Moreover, the English were Europe's leading gunfounders by the 1570s, and could equip their ships with cannon that outranged their foes.

This is not to say larger galleons were not built. *Ark Royal*, the flagship of the English fleet during the Armada campaign, displaced 800 tons. *White Bear* and *Dreadnought*, two other contemporary English galleons, displaced 1,000 tons and 1,100 tons, respectively. Yet even these were handier than Spanish galleons.

A period illustration showing a race-built Elizabethan galleon. Note the low forecastle, and the height of the gun deck above the water. Armed with culverins and properly handled, it could defeat a larger Spanish galleon due to its superior mobility. (Author's collection)

GOLDEN HIND

Estimated dimensions[1]

Tons burthen: 100–150 tons
Length of deck: 100ft
Breadth: 20ft
Draft: 10ft 6in.
Crew (initial): 80 men

[1] These dimensions are estimates and approximations. No measurements were made during its lifetime, and all depictions of its appearance are conjectural.

Golden Hind was built at Deptford in 1577 as *Pelican*. It was renamed *Golden Hind* in 1578, during Drake's voyage around the world. It became the first ship to circumnavigate the globe, and the first to complete the voyage under a single commander.

It was built as a commercial undertaking, rather than as a royal ship. It served as the flagship of the expedition, under Francis Drake's command. The expedition was a joint-stock venture, financed primarily by merchant investors, with the queen participating. Besides capturing *Nuestra Señora de la Concepción*, *Golden Hind* took several other ships, and was the ship that raided Spanish ports in the Pacific.

Golden Hind returned to England with treasure valued between £337,000 and £1.5 million. This included six tons of cloves, purchased in the Spice Islands (Maluku) after *Golden Hind* had crossed the Pacific on its way back to Plymouth.

Golden Hind never sailed again after completing Drake's voyage. At Queen Elizabeth's request, it was placed on permanent display as a museum ship at Deptford. Eventually, it was placed ashore. It remained in Deptford until around 1650, by which point it had finally rotted away.

THE STRATEGIC SITUATION

In 1550, neither Spain nor England were truly seafaring nations. Spain was a maritime power and had one of the largest navies in Europe, but it viewed its navy as a means of transporting armies and returning treasures from overseas possessions: the sea was a necessary evil. England was agrarian, despite the growth of industry in its south, and its economy largely depended upon the export of wool. It had ships, and as an island nation, was even more dependent upon shipping than Spain. Yet it, too, viewed ships as a means of transportation, not as a way to project power.

Spain was significantly wealthier than England in 1550. The Iberian Peninsula, containing Spain and Portugal, lay on Europe's south-west corner, making these nations ideally placed to sail by sea to the East Indies. Portugal explored south and east, and Spain went west. In the 1490s, both nations discovered a sea route to riches: Portugal rounded Africa's Cape of Good Hope, opening a route to India and the Spice Islands, while Spain discovered the New World – North and South America.

Both discoveries made their nations rich. But where Portugal was trading for African gold and Eastern spices and silks, Spain conquered indigenous empires in Central and South America, plundering vast amounts of gold and gems. The new territories they controlled also contained massive amounts of silver. Spain was mining so much silver that its value against gold dropped 50 per cent between 1450 and 1550, and a further 33 per cent over the next 100 years.

Moreover, this wealth was limited to Spain and Portugal. In 1494, at the urging of Pope Alexander VI, Spain and Portugal signed the Treaty of Tordesillas, which divided newly discovered lands outside Europe between the two Iberian nations at a point 370 leagues west of the Cape Verde Islands. Spain received a monopoly on all lands west of the line, Portugal a monopoly on all lands east of it. All other European nations were excluded from these territories. The treaty was ratified in 1506 by Pope Julius II, giving Catholic approval to the division. Other nations violating the monopolies risked excommunication.

Spain and England were nominal allies in 1550. Unlike England's friendship with Portugal, which started in the 14th century and was maintained by trade, the English–Spanish alliance was a marriage of convenience, spurred by a mutual distrust of France. The boy king Edward VII ruled England, while the aged Charles II headed the Habsburg Empire.

All that changed within six years. Edward died, to be succeeded by his oldest sister Mary Tudor, who became Queen Mary I of England. In 1556, Charles II abdicated in favour of his son, who ruled the sprawling Habsburg possessions of Spain, the Netherlands, Burgundy, Milan, Naples, Sicily and the Spanish overseas territories, including the Americas and Philippines. He had also been made sovereign of the Netherlands by his father the previous year, and it remained his favourite.

Philip and Mary had married two years earlier, in 1554. This further cemented the Anglo-Spanish alliance – in theory. England had become a Protestant nation in 1534, when Henry VIII separated the English church from papal authority. When Mary became queen in 1553, she attempted to bring England back into the Catholic fold, supported by her husband. Her attempts were coercive and heavy-handed, including the execution of those clinging to Protestant beliefs. By the time of her death in 1558, she had alienated many of her English subjects, who dubbed her Bloody Mary. She had also turned much of England against Catholicism.

Mary was replaced by her younger sister Elizabeth. Queen Elizabeth (she did not become Elizabeth I until Elizabeth II was crowned 400 years later) was Protestant, and was also willing to serve as the Protestant champion, at least for the form of Protestantism espoused by the Church of England. Unlike her father and sister, she proved relatively tolerant of other beliefs, sought a middle way between Catholicism and extreme Protestantism and was unwilling to sponsor the active persecution of heretics.

This put Spain and England on opposite sides of the religious wars ignited by the Reformation and Counter-Reformation. Despite strategic interests in remaining allies, the nations first drifted apart, and then into war in the decade following Elizabeth's coronation.

Although she described herself as possessing 'the body of a weak, feeble woman', Queen Elizabeth I of England proved indeed to have 'the heart and stomach of a king, and of a king of England too'. During her reign, she served as champion of the Protestant cause. (Library of Congress)

OPPOSITE
His Most Catholic Majesty Philip II ruled Spain and Spanish Habsburg territories from 1556 until his death in 1598. Throughout his reign, he served as Catholicism's principle champion. This painting shows him at the time of his marriage to Queen Mary I of England. (Author's collection)

29

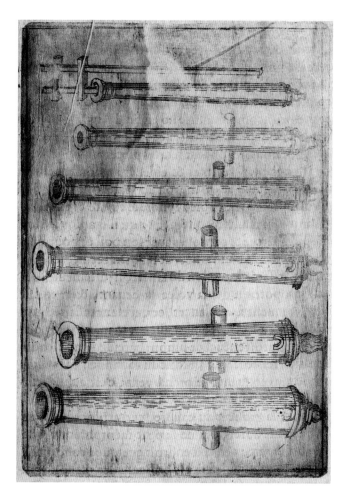

A page illustrating different types of 16th-century breechloading bronze artillery, taken from *Modelles, Artifices de Fev, et Divers Instrvmes de Gverre*, an artillery manual written by Joseph Boillot, published in France in 1598. Artillery changed land and sea warfare. (Author's collection)

Even before Elizabeth's accession, English sailors were defying the declared monopoly on trade to the Indies, Africa and the New World. The year before Mary's death, a West Country shipowner, John Hawkins, took a three-ship expedition to Africa, trading for slaves, selling the slaves in the Americas to willing Spanish buyers and then buying luxury products with the proceeds. He bought so many goods that he chartered two additional ships to carry everything to England. The two chartered ships were seized when they stopped in Spain, but profits from the three ships arriving in England yielded handsome profits. Hawkins soon embarked on a second voyage.

The road to war accelerated in 1567, when Philip II sent an army to the Netherlands to enforce Catholicism. Within a year, this sparked a rebellion in the Protestant north, the seven provinces that make up modern Netherlands. Philip initially succeeded in suppressing the rebellion, but in 1572, the rebels captured Brill. Most of Holland and Zeeland joined the rebels, and William the Silent, Prince of Orange was declared *Stadtholder*, head of the rebel cause.

That year, Hawkins led a third trading expedition to the Americas. This one had five ships, including two crown ships: *Minion* and *Jesus of Lubeck*. Another ship in the voyage, *Judith*, owned by Hawkins, was captained by a cousin, the then-unknown Francis Drake.

The third expedition ended in disaster. The English were trapped at San Juan de Ulúa on Mexico's coast by a Spanish fleet. Only *Minion* and *Judith* escaped: *Jesus of Lubeck* and the other two ships were captured. The events led to a redesign of English galleons. The race-built galleon was developed from Hawkins's experience at the battle, and a surge of shipbuilding followed.

San Juan de Ulúa also made Elizabeth more willing to turn a blind eye to English piracy against Spanish shipping. She began issuing letters of marque and reprisal, allowing English ships to redress losses due to Spain's actions by seizing Spanish ships and raiding Spanish colonies.

By 1577, Elizabeth was subsidizing the Dutch rebellion. That year, Drake started his voyage, which culminated in his raid on Spain's American Pacific coast and his eventual circumnavigation of the world. When Philip claimed the throne of Portugal, England supported Don Antonio de Crato, who declared himself king. After Philip's army had chased Don Antonio out of Lisbon, England supported Antonio's pretendership at his base in the Azores.

Drake returned in September 1580, and the following year, the Spanish ambassador to England warned Philip of the danger of England's growing naval power. While war seemed impending, the two nations were officially at peace – except across the Treaty of Tordesillas line – where 'No peace beyond the line' was the key maxim. Elizabeth refrained from declaring war, however.

In 1585, Spain experienced crop failure. Despite her vast New World wealth, the nation had money problems due to increasingly larger military efforts, declaring bankruptcy in

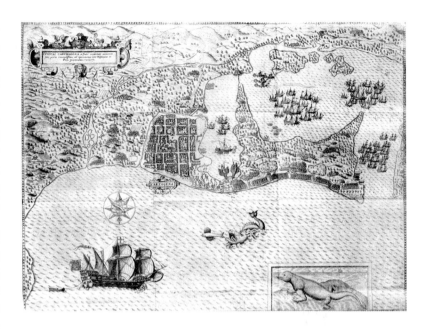

Following Philip II's seizure of English ships in Spanish ports in 1585, Elizabeth I authorized a massive raid on Spanish New World possessions between 1585 and 1586. Sir Francis Drake raided Cartagena de Indias (Colombia) in 1586, as shown in this print. The ship in the foreground is thought to be his flagship, *Bonaventure*. (Author's collection)

1575. Philip invited English ships to bring grain to Spain, guaranteeing immunity from restrictions on selling the cargoes in Spain. However, rather than paying for the grain, Philip ordered the seizure of the ships and the confiscation of the grain. Only one ship escaped to England.

War broke out at this point. Elizabeth commissioned a massive raid on Spain's American colonies, successfully led by Drake between 1585 and 1586. Elizabeth executed Mary, Queen of Scots (for supporting an assassination attempt on Elizabeth) in February 1587. This led Philip to plan an invasion of England to replace Elizabeth with a Catholic queen. The 1587 invasion was foiled by Drake, who raided the Spanish coast, preventing the fleet from assembling. Philip simply tried again in 1588, resulting in the Armada campaign.

While the invasion was prevented and the Spanish fleet destroyed, actual combat proved indecisive. Most of Spain's losses occurred due to shipwreck on the return home. The war did not end, however. Spain had the resources to build a new navy along the lines of England's race-built galleons. Between 1589 and 1591, Spain built 12 new large galleons, known as the Twelve Apostles, to form the core of a new and permanent Spanish navy.

Elizabeth sponsored expeditions against Spain in the following years. Many were commercial ventures underwritten by England's wealthy. Some, like the 1589 and 1592 expeditions to the Azores, were successful. The loot from the latter expedition equalled half of England's annual revenues. Others, like the 1591 Azores expedition, Drake's final 1595 New World expedition and the final 1597 Island Expedition (again to the Azores) were failures.

The decade following the Armada was the golden age of the English Sea Dogs: over 300 Portuguese and Spanish ships were captured by English privateers. It turned England into a truly seafaring nation, and devastated Spain's merchant marine, even as the flow of silver to Spain increased. The war continued until it was settled by the Treaty of London in August 1604.

NAVIGATION

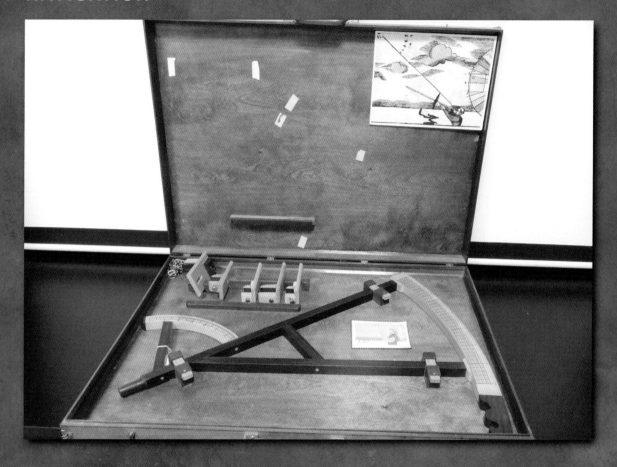

A replica of a Davis quadrant or backstaff, in the collection of the Houston Maritime Museum, for measuring the altitude of the sun using the projection of a shadow. (Houston Maritime Museum; author's photograph)

During the Middle Ages, most navigation was done by dead reckoning – estimating how fast you were going over a set period of time – and landmarks. The compass emerged during the 14th century, but coastal sailing for only short distances over open water was preferred.

For trans-oceanic voyages, navigators took ships to the latitude of the desired landfall, and sailed due east or west until land appeared. Dead reckoning estimated the distance travelled, and the compass ensured you sailed the right course.

To determine latitude, navigators measured the angle between the horizon and a point in the sky: Polaris at night and the sun during the day. Latitude was determined using a variety of instruments – the astrolabe, quadrant and backstaff. The high-tech tool for determining latitude was the Davis quadrant, invented by John Davis in 1594. Shown above, it allowed accurate measurement of the sun's altitude when it was up to 60 degrees above the horizon. It doubled the angle achievable by the standard quadrant, and could always be used accurately above 30 degrees north and below 30 degrees south.

TECHNICAL SPECIFICATIONS

THE HULL

Galleons were built from wood. The hulls were largely oak: gall oak in Spain, and white oak in England were the preferred timbers. Spanish galleons originally were constructed in Spain, mostly in two areas: the Basque country on the eastern edge of Spain's northern coast, and Andalusia, the province bordering Spain's southern coast. In England, much of the construction centred on the Channel coast or on the River Thames. These areas were then rich in mature oaks capable of providing ship timber. The European timber shortage would not occur for another two centuries.

Construction started with the keel – a large, straight, rectangular timber that formed the base of the hull. A single piece of wood was preferred. Since the keels of most galleons were less than 100ft long, this was usually achievable. Alternatively, two timbers were used, scarphed together.

Once the keel was laid down, the sternpost and stem were added. Both had the same cross-section as the keel. The sternpost was a straight piece of wood, raked back. The stem was made from compass timber (curved sections of oak), scarphed together, and was cut to a template. Both the sternpost and stem were critical elements of the ship's structure: the rudder hung off the sternpost, and the stem defined the bow's shape.

This model of a late-period Spanish galleon illustrates the Spanish propensity to build high forecastles on these vessels. While the high forecastle offered advantages during boarding actions, it made Spanish galleons harder to turn, because it acted as a fixed, immobile sail. (Houston Maritime Museum; author's photograph)

After this, the ship was framed. The master frame, at the ship's widest point, was added first. It defined the ship's breadth and depth of hold. Its shape would be sketched out on the floor of the mould loft (a large space where parts of the ship were drawn out in their proper dimensions), and the frame built by joining three to four timbers that had been cut to match the shape. The pairs of frames (port and starboard) were then added to the keel. Additional frames were added at intervals on the keel from the master frame, forward to the bow and aft to the stern. These would also be built in the mould loft, the shapes drawn on its floor according to formulae developed by the shipbuilder.

Plans were not used, and models infrequently so. Generally, the master shipwright was given the desired dimensions of the ship, and developed the frames through a combination of set guidelines and formulae, and his previous shipbuilding experience. Frame-building was still relatively new in the 16th century. Shipbuilding books were beginning to be published – some of the earliest appeared in the 15th century – but most naval architecture was learned through apprenticeship and experience.

The stern could have either a round tuck, where the planking went to the sternpost, or a square tuck. In this, the planking went to an after frame, and the stern had a flat transom across the after frame. The square tuck offered more space aft and a place to mount stern chasers, and became more popular throughout the 16th century.

Reinforcing elements were added to strengthen the hull. This included a mast step, a thick piece of wood with a morticed gap for the mainmast, placed atop the keel amidships. Seats for the pumps were installed next to the mast step. Deck beams, running athwart the ship, secured by wooden knees attached to the frames, were added next. Deck beams on gun decks, including the upper deck, were spaced closer than beams on decks intended only for stores or berthing. Finally, on the top of the stem, a heavy beam was placed that projected outwards and upwards to support the ship's beakhead.

Once the ship had been framed, it was planked. The planking was of oak, 1–3in. thick and 6–12in. wide, bent to match the frame. A few top strakes were added, and then planking began at the keel, working upwards. Thicker and wider planks, called wales, were added where extra strength was needed: at the turn of the bilge, the waterline and deck levels.

Ships were generally pegged together with wooden dowels, called treenails (pronounced 'trunnels'). These worked better than iron fittings, which corroded in seawater. Treenails swelled when wet, increasing their effectiveness.

The resulting hull was remarkably sturdy. It could support the weight of guns, withstand the fury of the seas and survive beaching (as these ships occasionally were, to clean their bottoms).

THE GUNS

Wrought iron guns were falling out of favour by 1550. The English continued using them through to 1570, and the Spanish – due to shortages of better, cast artillery to replace them – used them until at least 1590. Those in remote locations, where replacement was difficult, endured the longest. They were called lombards or bombards in Spain, or port pieces and slings in England, depending on size (lombards and port guns were bigger), but can generically be referred to as bombards.

Bombards had bores that ranged from 3in. to 7½in., and a total length (barrel and chamber) between 9½ft and 10½ft. The carriage, typically a cradle with a sturdy back

Three Spanish bombards, recovered from the *San Esteban*. The foreground item is a replica sledge carriage. While obsolescent by 1550 and obsolete by 1590, Spain continued using them due to shortages of better artillery. (William Lardas)

FIRING A BREECHLOADING CANNON

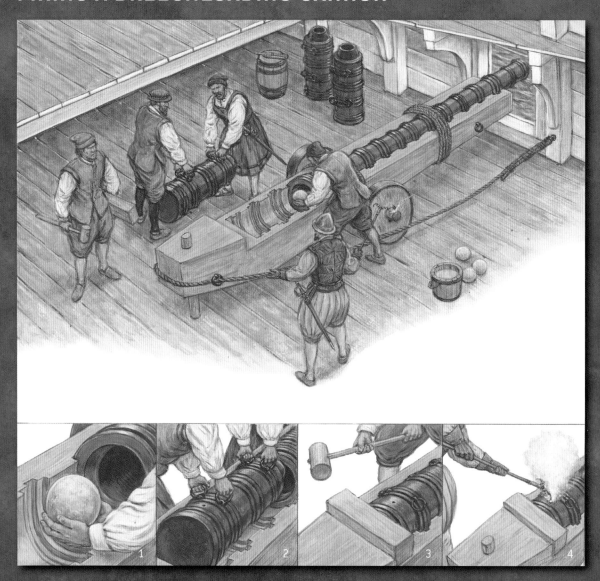

Breechloading cannon of the 16th century were loaded in a manner different to naval muzzleloaders.

1. The first step was to place a cannonball at the back of the tube of the cannon. Next, the gunner charged the chamber with the appropriate measure of gunpowder.

2. Two members of the crew then placed the chamber behind the tube barrel. The chamber had rings to allow it to be carried. The back of the chamber was closed, and so it was carried angled with the back down, to prevent gunpowder from spilling out.

3. Once the chamber was in place, a third crew member took a wooden wedge, hammering it between the back of the carriage and the back of the chamber. This provided a tight seal between the tube and the chamber.

4. The gunner would add priming powder to the chamber's touchhole, stand to one side and light the priming. This fired the cannon.

After firing, the block was hammered out, allowing the chamber to be removed. Loading and firing would be repeated with a new chamber, while the old one cooled.

piece to restrain the chamber, added another 3ft to the length of the gun. These guns were not intended to recoil. The Spanish often mounted these guns on immovable sledge carriages. The English preferred a two-wheel carriage, but these were intended to allow the guns to be shifted, not to recoil.

These guns usually fired stone shot typically weighing between 3 lb and 10 lb. Individual guns typically had multiple chambers, two or three per gun. The ball was placed in the barrel, and the powder charge, measured by the gunner, was placed in the chamber. The chamber had rings to allow it to be lifted and lowered into the carriage.

Cast guns were more common by the 1570s, being more powerful, easier to make and safer. These were muzzleloading smoothbores. Cast bronze was preferred over cast iron during the 16th century, largely because it was easier to cast bronze without cracks or voids (which made a gun more likely to explode when fired); bronze, however, conducted heat better and annealed, softening the metal, if the gun got too hot.

Cracks and voids were formed by pouring the metal used for the gun when it was too cool, whether bronze or iron. Better methods of heating iron developed during the last half of the 16th century, yet throughout the 16th century cast bronze remained the preferred choice.

It was easier to standardize cast artillery sizes than wrought iron guns. Standardization meant the same balls could be used in all guns of a similar size aboard ship, simplifying logistics. By 1550, the standard cast cannon used aboard ship were as follows (the weight of iron shot fired by these guns is given in parentheses following the name of the gun): the demi-cannon (32 lb), culverin (18 lb), basilisk (14 lb), demi-culverin (8 lb), saker (6 lb), minion (5¼ lb) and falcon (2 lb).

The demi-cannon and culverins had barrels between 10ft and 11ft long and weighed between 4,000 lb and 5,000 lb. Only the bore was fully standardized. The lengths and weights for these guns varied and culverins were often cast heavier and longer than demi-cannon. The demi-culverin was between 8ft and 9ft long and weighed between 3,000lb and 3,500 lb. Smaller guns, sakers, minions and falcons were between 6ft and 7ft long. Sakers weighed around 1,500 lb, minions around 1,000 lb and falcons between 650 lb and 700 lb.

These were all carriage-mounted, on four-wheel trucks in English ships, and on field carriages in Spanish. There were also smaller cannon mounted on swivels. These included the falconet (1 lb shot), serpentine (8 oz. shot) and the rabinet (4 oz. shot). They fired both iron and lead shot.

A cutaway of a 16th-century bronze muzzleloading cannon, from the 16th-century Italian artillery manual *Perfeto Bombardiero et Real Instruttione di Artiglier*. This cannon has a chamber (the reduced diameter in the bore shown between 'A' and 'S') for the gunpowder, which was thought to improve the thrust on the cannonball. (Author's collection)

CANNON AMMUNITION

Replicas of 16th-century artillery ammunition. (Author's collection)

While the standard ammunition used in naval cannon during this period was the solid ball, other specialized rounds were used aboard ship, including chain shot and grapeshot.

Ball shot (lower left in the picture) was a solid ball, sometimes made from stone, but by the time of the Armada mostly cast from iron. Iron balls were heavier than stone of the same size, and were easier to produce in quantity in a uniform size. Ball shot was used to batter a ship's timbers.

Grapeshot (lower right) consisted of several layers of small ball shot tied together with cord, typically with a cloth wrapping, sitting on a wooden base the diameter of the gun. The cord and cloth burned off and the shot scattered. It was an anti-personnel weapon.

Chain shot (upper left) comprised two balls linked together by a short chain. Its primary use was to cut rigging and to break spars or (fired at short range) even small masts, but it was also effective against people.

These are replicas, displayed on *El Galeón Andalucia*, a modern reconstruction of a Spanish galleon.

These small cannon were included in a ship's gun count. A ship carrying 42 guns might have 22 culverins, six sakers and 14 falconets and serpentines. The collection of small guns fired a broadside equal to one culverin.

The British favoured the culverin in a galleon's main battery. These guns had a longer range than the heavier guns due to a longer length-to-bore ratio. The 18 lb shot was a manageable size, given the way guns were then loaded. They were not run in and reloaded inboard, as they would be later, because there was not enough room in a ship to allow this. The guns could only be run in enough to close the gunports. Rather, the gunner straddled the gun, leaning at least his upper body outside the ship to swab out the gun after it had fired, and to reload it. It was easier to load an 18 lb ball than a 32 lb ball this way. This was a major reason for the slow rate of fire during the 16th century.

Two types of gunpowder were used in this era: serpentine powder and corned powder. In serpentine powder, the ingredients (saltpetre, sulphur and charcoal) were finely ground and mixed. This produced a slow-burning powder that required a long gun barrel, to ensure the powder was completely burnt by the time the shot exited the bore. In corned powder, the ingredients were dissolved and ground into grains. This was faster burning, resulting in greater power: corned powder was 50 per cent more powerful than serpentine powder. Corned powder began to be widely used by the middle of the century.

THE RIGGING

By 1550, the galleon developed a standard configuration of masts, spars and sails that it retained through to the end of the century. While extra sails and upper masts were added over time, these tended to be variations or extensions of conventional practice.

The standard mast configuration from front to back consisted of a bowsprit, foremast, mainmast and mizzenmast. A bonaventure mast was occasionally added aft of the mizzen. Only the mainmast went down to the ship's keel, where it was secured (stepped). The bowsprit and remaining masts were deck stepped. The bowsprit was frequently stepped at the forward orlop platform. The foremast was generally stepped at the gun deck, and the mizzen at the upper deck. The bonaventure, when permanent, was usually stepped one deck below the topmost deck of the sterncastle.

The bowsprit was generally set at a 45-degree angle from the horizontal, but the angle could vary, depending on the captain's preferences. It served several functions. It held the forestays that kept the foremast from falling backwards. It was also used for the bowlines, which controlled the foresails. It also held a spar for a square sail, the spritsail, hung below the bowsprit and used to help turn the ship. There was no jibboom in the 16th century. The bowsprit was a bare pole.

Behind the bowsprit was the foremast, which carried square sails. At the time, it was generally set at a forward rake up to 15 degrees from the vertical. The central mainmast was best stepped at the longitudinal pivot point of the hull. The mainmast, too, had square sails, whereas the mizzen and bonaventure masts carried lateen sails. These triangular sails were attached to a long spar hung diagonally on the mast.

A characteristic of mainsail and foresail spars during the 16th century was this double-spar arrangement, where the starboard and larboard yards were lashed together over the middle third of the span. The lower yard was carved out to allow the upper yard to fit snugly. By the 17th century, the two halves were scarphed together, making them appear like a single piece. (Houston Maritime Museum; author's photograph)

By 1550, galleons carried multiple sails on the fore- and mainmasts. The upper sails, which were also square, were hung from upper masts attached to the lower masts. Attached ahead of the lower mast was the topmast, which was joined at the mast top to the lower mast. On large galleons, especially late in the 16th century, a third mast was mounted at the top of the topmast, ahead of the topmast, called the topgallant mast.

Only the lowest masts were permanently fixed. The spars and (late in the 16th century) upper masts could be removed and lowered to the deck. This reduced leverage in high winds, keeping the ship from heeling excessively in a beam wind, and the masts from breaking in a following wind. Excessive heel slowed a ship, reducing its depth and making the ship leewardly – subject to being pushed sideways by wind, instead of ahead.

The sails carried the name of the mast to which their spars hung: fore- or mainsail for the lowest sail on the lowest mast segment of those masts; fore or main topsail for the sail on the topmast; and topgallant sail for the sail hung from the topgallant mast. The lower sails were rectangular. The topsails and topgallants were trapezoidal, the width of the lower spar at the bottom and the width of the upper spar at the top. The lower sails still provided the main driving force for a galleon, but the topsails contributed a significant amount to a ship's speed.

The lateen mizzen and bonaventure masts could also have topmasts. A lateen sail, typically one-third the surface area of the lower sail, could serve as a topmast. These were rarely used at sea. Often, even if a mizzen topmast was set, the spar for its mizzen was stored on the deck.

Two things restricted the growth of and dependence on upper sails: the lack of footropes, and the inability to shorten these sails. A footrope was a line attached under the spar. It was set so a sailor standing on the footrope had the spar at waist height. He could bend over the spar, providing stability as he worked the sail. They did not appear until the middle of the 17th century. A galleon sailor had to crawl out on the spar, legs wrapped around it. This was unstable and made working aloft on the spar dangerous, especially in high winds.

Reef points (lines of ropes along the width of the sail that could be tied around the spar to shorten the sail's length) also lay in the future. Instead, sails were lengthened by adding bonnets, rectangular strips laced to the bottom of the sail. The line was interlaced, so cutting one loop at the end of the sail allowed the bonnet to 'unzip' and be carried away in an emergency. Bonnets were attached by lowering the spar so the bottom of the sail grazed the deck, where the bonnet was then attached. This meant bonnets were only practical for the fore- and mainsail. Foresails had one bonnet, while the mainsail generally could attach a second bonnet under the upper bonnet.

Footropes did not appear until the middle of the 17th century. Footropes under the yard allowed sailors a place to stand while they leaned on the yard near their waists. The absence of footropes (as shown here) made work aloft highly dangerous. (Houston Maritime Museum; author's photograph)

CHANGING SAIL AREA

Without footropes and reef points, there were only limited ways to adjust the amount of sail a ship carried to match the wind conditions. Instead of reducing the size of sails by reefing them, lower sails were smaller than subsequent forms. Canvas was added, in strips called bonnets, laced into the bottom of the sail.

A. The spar was lowered until the sail's bottom touched the deck.

B. A strip of rope, the lacing, ran along the sail's bottom, with loops pushed through eyelets. Sailors pushed a loop through the corresponding eyelet on the bonnet and passed through the previous loop, interlocking them. The final loop was lashed to the corner of the sail.

C. One means of reducing the sail area was goose-winging. Three lines controlled a sail's bottom corner: the sheet, tack and clewline. When the sail area needed to be reduced, the sheet and tack were loosened, and the clewline, which ran to the spar, was drawn up until the corner reached the spar. This reduced the sail area to three half-ovals, which roughly resembled the outspread wing of a goose.

D. Work aloft without footropes was dangerous. The sailor shown here has to cut away the sail, which is endangering the ship in high winds. He has to crawl out on the spar, wrapping his arms and legs around it, and hope he does not fall off when he uses one hand to cut the robands tying the sail to the spar.

THE COMBATANTS

In James Boswell's *Life of Johnson*, Samuel Johnson states: 'No man will be a sailor who has contrivance enough to get himself into jail; for being in a ship is being in a jail, with the chance of being drowned.' Johnson made that pronouncement in the mid-18th century, yet it was just as true two centuries earlier. Or perhaps even truer.

Life aboard ship in the period 1550–1605 was wretched and deadly. Expeditions sailed with hundreds of men, but returned with only scores of survivors. For example, Drake's circumnavigation set off with 156 aboard, and returned with 56. In Magellan's circumnavigation in 1519, of the 270 sailors departing Spain, a mere 18 survived. Both of the commanders that feature in this book's biographies died of disease at sea.

Despite the dangers, most men participating in these ventures, whether as privateers and pirates or aboard national warships, signed on willingly. Only in rare cases – such as the Enterprise of England, when Spain sent a fleet of 130 ships against England – was conscription used. Even then, most sailors conscripted were the crews of merchant vessels impressed into service, and were treated as part of the movable fittings of the ship.

Some volunteered because they lacked other choices: they could go to sea, or starve. Others came from seagoing families. Many chose to man privateers and warships from a sense of adventure, knowing a trip aboard a privateering venture offered an opportunity for advancement that would be impossible on land. This turn of the wheel of fortune could make a man rich, whether he joined the venture as a prosperous gentleman or an impoverished farm labourer. It rewarded competence, and the lucky. A lowly born, impoverished youngster could rise to command and to wealth with sufficient ambition, hard work and luck. You might die of disease or injury at sea, but, equally, that was often the fate of those who remained on land.

Mariners were among the few people in the 16th century who travelled more than 30 miles from their homes – and their horizons were defined only by how far their ships sailed. This shows *Golden Hind* in the Mariana Islands in 1579, half a world distant from its starting port of Plymouth. (Author's collection)

THE SAILORS

In the 16th century, sailors of all sides were remarkably homogeneous. Whether English, Spanish or from any of the countries in Europe, the main differences between them tended to be the language they spoke, the religion they practised and the foods they preferred.

Differences in religions often were significant (this was the period of the religious wars of the Protestant Reformation and Catholic Counter-Reformation). Yet the language and dietary differences were easily bridged. Wherever they came from, sails, rigging and masting were similar enough to be recognizable by any experienced mariner. So were duties: steering the ship, raising and lowering the anchors, manning pumps and handling the ships' boats. Handling the great guns was a technique easily learned, although loading, aiming and firing them required both skill and experience. Similarly, piracy was so endemic that even civilian sailors knew how to handle boarding weapons, such as pikes and swords.

Common sailors – the men whose primary responsibility was to handle and sail a ship – tended to belong to one of three categories: seamen, apprentices and ships' boys. The seamen were experienced sailors, the apprentices were adults (although frequently in their late teens) learning to become sailors and the ships' boys were lads aged between 8 and 14 whose responsibilities were largely those of servants.

Given the small size of typical warships, 400 tons or less, the sailors aboard a warship might run from 30 to 60 men. Aboard the 1,000-ton *San Martín*, only 177 of its crew of 500 were sailors, the rest being gunners or soldiers.

An experienced sailor was called a *marinero* in Spain, and a seaman in England. They corresponded to the 'able seaman' rating of the Napoleonic-era Royal Navy. These men knew which ropes controlled which sails, and were capable of shortening sail (by removing bonnets in this era – reef points were not used until footropes appeared) and steering the ship by manning the wheel or tiller. They could also read a compass and mark the ship's progress on a chart. They typically had more than three years' experience as a sailor, and formed the backbone of the crew.

Apprentices (called *grumetes* in Spain) were the men learning the trade of seamanship. There was no concept of a landsman at this time. Even the greenest hand, one straight off the farm, signed on as an apprentice. Their primary duties were handling the sails, manning the capstan or windlass when raising and lowering the anchor and pulling lines on the guns. They were the ones used when strong backs and nimble limbs were needed, and they often worked under the seamen's leadership. They were typically younger men, often between the ages of 16 and 19, and usually had fewer than three years' experience as sailors. While a dull individual might remain an apprentice for years, those who showed ability were promoted to seaman or mariner after three years.

Ships' boys (called pages in England, or *pajes* in Spain) served the officers, cleaned cabins, swept the decks and set the mess tables. They sang hymns to encourage the

English sailors aboard a galleon. While language and religion differed, mariners, regardless of nationality, dressed in a similar manner and mastered the same sets of skills. Whether Spaniard, Englishman, Dutchman, Frenchman or Venetian, a sailor would find himself at home on any nation's ships. (Author's collection)

A topman climbing to the masthead of a Spanish ship. The sailors who worked in the tops were generally in their mid- to late teens, aged 15 to 18. By that age, they were strong enough for the work, but still light enough and possessing the agility for work aloft. (Author's collection)

crew, and also stood standard watches alongside them, being responsible for watching and turning the sandglass, to keep track of time. As they grew older, they typically followed one of two tracks. Those who were born into the gentry or nobility, or boys of humble background, who impressed one of the ship's officers, might move onto the track of becoming a ship's officer. Those without family connections generally became apprentice seamen when old enough.

Ideally, 90 per cent of a ship's company would be evenly split between seamen and apprentices, with the remaining 10 per cent made up of ships' boys. A ship required specialists, and the more experienced and capable seamen moved into these positions of greater authority and skill.

A quartermaster or bosun was responsible for management of the rigging and sails and ground tackle, and the placement of the crew. He was also responsible for the ship's lading (loading), and needed to be literate to manage the paperwork associated with inventory and cargo.

The ship's carpenter and caulker saw to the soundness of the hull. The carpenter did the woodworking aboard the ship, including repairing battle damage or replacing rotten timbers. He was also responsible for replacing blocks and sheaves (pulley wheels). The caulker ensured the ship remained relatively watertight. His responsibilities included ensuring a ship's hull was properly sealed with tallow, pitch and caulk prior to the voyage, and plugging leaks at sea. Similarly, the cooper looked after the barrels used to store provisions. He stopped any leaks that were found, and, if necessary, could make new barrels.

A steward (called a *despensero* aboard Spanish ships) saw to the allocation of food and provisions. He tracked wine and water storage, and supervised the cooking of meals, aided by the ship's boys. Over time, as ships grew larger, his duties split into the separate roles of cook and purser.

Finally, there was a barber-surgeon responsible for the crew's health. This included cutting hair, and (when necessary) cutting off limbs. He also dispensed medicine, and treated illnesses at sea. Barber-surgeons typically lacked any formal training during this period, and picked up the skills required through experience.

Unlike soldiers, neither British nor Spanish sailors enlisted for fixed terms: they signed on for a single voyage, and were discharged at its end. This was true for naval warships, privateers and merchant vessels. The voyage might last a month or two for a coastal trader, or up to three years for a naval warship. Since navies commissioned warships for specific purposes and rarely kept large fleets standing in commission, the system worked.

THE OFFICERS

In this period, there were two command structures in a warship: officers concerned with the navigation and management of the ship; and officers commanding the soldiers and gunners aboard, and the ship, in battle. This tradition was centuries old, dating to pre-gunpowder times. When the crown wanted warships, it drafted merchant ships and kept the crews (including the navigation officers and ships' masters), while appointing its own officers to command the ship and the soldiers sent to it.

At the beginning of the period, the ship's captain on a warship belonged to the latter category. English or Spanish, he was a soldier first and a mariner second. One difference between Spanish and English captains was that this changed over time. By 1600, most English captains were as much mariners as warriors, having evolved from soldiers at sea to naval officers.

The change was due to England's poverty and Spain's wealth. Except during active warfare, Elizabeth's navy had few warships in commission. Most fighting English warships were privateers or pirates, operating as private ventures run by civilian subjects of the crown. These ships were captained by their owners, or a man appointed by the syndicate outfitting the ship. The man commanding the ship could navigate and fulfil the role of ship's master as well as leading the fighting. The outstanding example of this was Drake, who evolved from a merchant captain with no military background to one of England's admirals; but there were many other such captains in England.

Spain did not depend on privateers. It fought with national warships, commissioned by the crown, with officers appointed by the king. These officers were picked for their loyalty to the king and their presumed fidelity to the mission they were assigned. Sailing the ship was a

Pages or *pajes* made up around 10 per cent of the crew on both English and Spanish ships. Their duties included cleaning the ship, serving meals and leading hymns. They were frequently the butt of jokes. (Author's collection)

A sea officer, Spanish or English, could be identified by command presence, and the higher quality of his clothing and weapons. Officers were expected to be 'gently born', although exemplary commoners could rise to command. (Author's collection)

secondary consideration, and could be left to maritime professionals. Familiarity with the sea was useful, but in caste-conscious Spain, less important than being of higher nobility than any other officer aboard.

Over time, this favoured England. English captains were more familiar with the tools of naval combat than their Spanish adversaries. They used their ships more effectively than their Spanish counterparts, who often missed seeing opportunities due to inexperience, and were forced to spend time consulting the ship's master and pilot before reaching conclusions. In modern parlance, the English captains operated inside the decision loop of the Spanish.

As with the sailors manning the ships, the ships' officers (English or Spanish) commanding the crews and soldiers came from backgrounds more alike than different. Most were 'gently born', descended from knights, the landed gentry or the nobility. The exception was the rare common sailor who, through sheer ability, rose to high command.

In both societies, blood mattered more than ability. The nobles supported and advised the monarch, and the gentry supported the nobility. The Rights of Man and belief in the ability of the commoner lay two centuries in the future; common folk were assumed to lack leadership ability. While Drake's humble origins are emphasized today, he was distantly related to Sir Bernard Drake, who had a coat of arms – pretentions to nobility. Similarly, Pedro Sarmiento de Gamboa was well born, but impoverished.

To be born impoverished was a common point of origin for future sea officers. Life at sea was dangerous, but service as a maritime officer was considered within the dignity of the well born and offered opportunities for wealth and honour difficult to find on land, other than in the army or government service. A man who lacked interest in an army or government career could always find an opening aboard a ship.

The officers concerned with operation and navigation were the master (*maestro* in Spanish) and the navigating officer, sometimes called a pilot (*piloto* in Spanish). The master filled the role traditionally thought of as captain. He was the 'master before

SIR FRANCIS DRAKE

Sir Francis Drake was the most famous of the Elizabethan Sea Dogs, a ship captain, privateer, naval officer and explorer. His most notable feat was the second circumnavigation of the world, during a three-year expedition starting in 1577, in which he captured the treasure ship *Nuestra Señora de la Concepción*.

Drake was born in 1540 (day and month unknown) in a cottage near Tavistock, Devon, the eldest of the 12 children of Edmond and Mary Drake. Little is known of Drake's youth. The family was poor, but not impoverished. Edmond, part of the gentry, was descended from a younger son of an influential family. His family was strongly Protestant when Devon was still largely Catholic. Drake's father, a farmer at Tavistock, fled with his family to Kent during the Prayer Book Rising in 1549, and there he became a minister.

Drake's father apprenticed Drake to a neighbour, who owned and captained a small coastal bark used for trading with France. When the man died, and lacking heirs, he willed the ship to Drake. Commanding this ship for a few years, Drake moved to more ambitious endeavours. In 1555 and 1556, he participated in trading voyages to Guinea and the Spanish Main, probably transporting slaves.

In 1567, commanding the 50-ton *Judith*, he participated in an ambitious, five-ship slave-trading expedition organized by John Hawkins, a cousin. Initially successful, the ships were at San Juan de Ulúa (modern Veracruz), with their cargoes sold and ready to return to England, when they were trapped and destroyed by a Spanish fleet. Of the seven English ships in port (a further two ships had joined the expedition), only Drake's *Judith* and the 100-ton *Minion*, commanded by Hawkins, escaped.

The Spanish launched their attack during a truce, fostering Drake's lifelong hatred of Spain. Between 1570 and 1573, Drake conducted a series of reconnaissance and raiding voyages to the Caribbean and Spanish Main, which left Spain poorer and Drake richer, making him a hero in England. He captured 20 tons of silver and gold from the Spanish silver train at Nombre de Dios on Panama's eastern coast.

Sir Francis Drake.
(Library of Congress)

His successes led Queen Elizabeth to issue Drake a formal commission of reprisal (making him a privateer) for his next expedition, a raid on Spain's Pacific coast. The expedition sailed on 15 November 1577 with the galleons *Pelican* (later renamed *Golden Hind* to honour Queen Elizabeth) and *Elizabeth*, and three smaller vessels: *Marigold*, *Swan* and *Christopher*.

The voyage took three years. The three smaller vessels were lost before reaching the Straits of Magellan, where *Elizabeth* turned back to England. Only *Golden Hind* reached the Pacific. The Spanish were almost defenceless, and Drake pillaged the coast from Valparaíso to Panama, capturing *Nuestra Señora de la Concepción* in the process. Rather than returning through the straits, Drake sailed across the Pacific, circumnavigating the globe, and returned to Plymouth in September 1580. The loot from the voyage made the investors rich. The queen's portion was greater than England's annual national debt. Elizabeth knighted Drake.

Following this voyage, Drake served as mayor of Plymouth and a member of parliament. When Spain declared war on England, Drake led a 21-ship raid on Spain in 1585, capturing and holding Vigo for two weeks before crossing the Atlantic and raiding the Cape Verde Islands, and numerous Spanish possessions in the Americas and Caribbean. In 1587, he raided Cadiz, delaying the planned Spanish invasion of England for a year.

In 1588, when the Spanish Armada finally sailed, Drake was one of the admirals commanding the English fleet. Commanding *Revenge*, he captured the *Nuestra Señora del Rosario* in single combat. Later, he helped organize the fireship attack that broke up the Spanish fleet.

In 1589, with John Norrys, he co-commanded an expedition against Spain, but was repulsed attacking Corunna. He led a final expedition against Spanish New World possessions in 1595, but had lost his touch. He experienced defeats at Las Palmas de Gran Canaria, San Juan in north-eastern Puerto Rico and Portobelo in Panama. Off Portobelo, he contracted dysentery and died on 28 January 1596. He was buried at sea there, in a lead coffin, in full armour.

PEDRO SARMIENTO DE GAMBOA

Pedro Sarmiento de Gamboa was better known as an explorer and navigator than as a fighting-ship captain, but over the course of his career, he did both. After Drake entered the Pacific, Sarmiento was the man commanding the fleet sent in search of the Englishman.

He came from a Galician family, in the north-west corner of Spain. Born at Alcalá de Henares around 1532, he was brought up in his father's home at Pontevedra, near Galicia's western coast. Sarmiento joined Spain's military service aged 18, and spent the period 1550–55 as a soldier, fighting in the various wars in Europe.

In 1556, he departed for New Spain, spending two years in Mexico and Guatemala before proceeding to Peru in 1557. He spent seven years in Peru, studying the Incas, and making several coastal voyages. This gave him an acquaintance with ships and navigation. He served as a minor official in Spain's viceregal court at Lima. In 1564, he fell afoul of the Inquisition and was imprisoned, but was freed after a successful appeal to the Pope.

In 1567, Sarmiento proposed an exploration expedition to Peru's governor, seeking new lands west of Peru. Named captain of *Los Reyes*, his ship left Callao, Peru, in 1567, accompanied by a second ship, the *Todos Santos*. Pedro de Ortega aboard *Todos Santos* served as the expedition's *almirante* (admiral), Sarmiento was in charge of determining the course of the expedition.

The expedition discovered the Solomon Islands, encountering Santa Isabel first in 1568. One island reminded Sarmiento of his home, so he named it Guadalcanal. The expedition found no gold, and failed to establish a colony. Upon returning to the Americas, on 23 January 1569 at Santiago de Colima, Mexico, Sarmiento left the expedition.

A new viceroy, Don Francisco de Toledo, arrived in November 1569. In 1572, he commissioned Sarmiento to write a history of the Incas. The resultant *History of the Incas* remains one of the most important primary sources of Incan history.

The Inquisition resumed persecution of Sarmiento in 1573, attempting to imprison him or banish him on several occasions over the next five years. However, he remained under the protection of Don Francisco, for whom Sarmiento was the viceroy's go-to man in military and naval emergencies.

Don Francisco tasked Sarmiento with stopping Drake after the latter's attack on Callao, Lima's port. Sarmiento assembled and hastily armed several ships, and set off in pursuit. His ships trailed Drake from the capture of *Nuestra Señora del Rosario* through to Drake's last raid at Huatulco, Mexico.

Losing touch with Drake in Mexico, Sarmiento headed south to catch Drake as he returned to the Atlantic with his loot. This failed, because Drake crossed the Pacific, returning home via the Indian Ocean. Instead, Sarmiento took his ships across the passage from west to east, arriving at Spain in 1580.

With Diego Flórez de Valdés, Sarmiento co-commanded an expedition to fortify the Straits of Magellan in 1581 to prevent a repeat of Drake's exploit. The expedition departed with 24 ships, but lost eight to storms and an additional 12 as Valdés returned to Spain with them. Sarmiento pressed on with the four remaining ships, establishing a 300-man settlement in the Straits of Magellan in January 1583.

Returning to Spain in 1584, he was captured by a fleet commanded by Walter Raleigh, and imprisoned in England. There he met with Queen Elizabeth. She had him carry a 'Letter of Peace' to King Philip of Spain in 1586, in an effort to forestall war. He was captured by Huguenot pirates en route, and the letter was never delivered. Eventually freed, he returned to Spain in 1591.

Gamboa spent the next few years writing, but took part in an expedition to the Philippines. He served there for several years, including leading an expedition to besiege a mutinous Spanish officer. He remained in the Philippines, dying in Manila in 1608.

Pedro Sarmiento de Gamboa.
(Raimundo Pastor, CC BY-SA 4.0)

God', the man responsible for the ship's operation, sailing and lading. He was frequently a good merchant. In days when ships switched between merchant vessels in peacetime and warships in wartime, he was usually the ship's owner (or the owner's representative). His peacetime job was ensuring the ship made a profit. On English ships, and some Spanish ships, he was also the navigator.

The navigating officer was generally the master's first mate on English ships, but on some Spanish ships the *piloto* was the only man who could navigate the ship. English navigators tended to learn navigation on the job. Spanish *pilotos* studied mathematics, navigation, spherical trigonometry and coastal piloting for three years before they could receive an appointment as a royal pilot aboard a Spanish crown ship.

The actual commander of a warship, the captain (*capitán* in Spain), was most often a military officer – a soldier who was either a nobleman, a close relative of a nobleman or someone who had convinced the crown to appoint him. In England, aboard a crown ship, the commander might also be a naval officer, especially after 1580. This man directed the ship in combat. The senior captain in a group of warships, if no admiral was appointed in command, often became the captain-general, and commanded all the ships. Senior frequently did not mean most experienced, but more often indicated the highest-ranking noble.

A final officer, only found on Spanish ships, was the *escribano* or *veedor real*, the crown's representative. He served as comptroller and paymaster. His job was to track expenditures and any money obtained (through capturing a ship or transporting treasure), and to ensure the crown got its percentage of the profits. A glorified accountant, to King Philip of Spain he was the most important man aboard.

Both sides carried contingents of soldiers aboard. The Spanish regularly employed soldiers from their tercios (infantry divisions) aboard their ships, such as these Spanish pikemen. (Author's collection)

SEA SOLDIERS

All warships of the period, whether privateers or naval warships, carried soldiers aboard to aid in the fighting. Although they filled the role marines would serve a century or two later, they were not marines, the latter being soldiers trained to fight aboard ship and to assist the sailors aboard the ships during battle.

Rather, they were most usually soldiers, trained for land warfare, temporarily placed aboard ship to fight. This was a hangover from earlier periods, when a warship was generally a merchant ship impressed into service with soldiers replacing paying cargo, and battle at sea meant boarding actions. Artillery was not yet thought of as a ship-killing weapon, or even the primary weapon in a sea battle. Its chief function was to assist the soldiers by weakening the enemy ship before the inevitable boarding action.

In this period, especially in Spain, gunners were considered part of the ship's military contingent. Mariners might be trusted to pull the gun tackles, but loading and aiming required knowledge and experience, and was only to be entrusted to trained specialists (a belief such specialists encouraged, to increase their value). A ship typically carried one gunner per two guns aboard, although no regulation controlled this.

The soldier contingent varied, depending upon nationality. The Spanish averaged 2.5 soldiers for every mariner aboard a ship. A ship manned by 100 mariners would thus carry 250 soldiers. As usual, this varied. Depending on the captain's preferences and the availability of soldiers, the ratio of mariners to soldiers aboard a ship ranged from 1:1 to 1:6. This ratio held only at the outset of a voyage: disease reduced the mariners and soldiers as the voyage progressed.

The English ships usually carried fewer soldiers than the Spanish ones, generally a ratio of one to two soldiers for every mariner. Part of the reason was expense and availability. On privateering voyages, soldiers shared the plunder, but did little of the seamanship. People also tended to die if crowded in too heavily. Having more than one person aboard per ton of ship's displacement tended to increase disease rates (a lesson learned through painful experience).

Moreover, many English warships were private ventures. The crown sent soldiers aboard national ships. Private ventures had to hire soldiers. Only if the queen hired the ship were soldiers provided. Even then, Queen Bess was cheeseparing and skimped on soldiers, for they had to be paid. Most private investors chose to hire extra sailors willing to fight as soldiers. Their pure soldiers tended to be 'gentleman adventurers', unsalaried volunteers paid only through a share of prize money.

Regardless of how they got aboard ship, the soldiers tended to be armed like, and fought like, their shore brethren. Relatively few wore full armour, as much due to expense as its cumbersome nature aboard, but helmets and breastplates were used. Leather jackets were more common, due to cost. Few worried about drowning due to the weight of armour: few knew how to swim, and would drown almost as quickly naked as in full plate.

Weapons tended to be land weapons cut down for naval use: swords, axes and half-pikes were among the most common. Long pole arms were useful for repelling boarders, but less handy for offensive operations: since capturing the enemy required boarding, they were of limited used. Missile weapons included arquebuses and crossbows. Longbows were too unwieldy for shipboard use, although they occasionally appeared. The crossbow was the most common weapon due to the expense of the arquebus, its slow rate of fire and vulnerability to damp.

Despite naval artillery, the contingent of soldiers was still seen as the decisive weapon in maritime combat in 1550. The weakness of bombards and lombards, still widely used in the mid-16th century, made this understandable. For much of the period covered, maritime hand-to-hand combat was little changed from the days of the Battle of Sluys two centuries earlier. Ships closed to missile range (arrow, quarrels and musket balls, with artillery thrown in for extra effect). After a brief exchange of fire, the ship that thought it was winning brought itself alongside its enemy, and fought a mêlée action. The boarders would take their prize, or be driven off to try again.

BOARDING WEAPONS

While there were national differences in the individual types of weapons, both used the same classes of weapons. The weapons are displayed here with Spanish items to the left, and English ones to the right.

Pole arms

1. Pikes had a steel-pointed end, and a long spear.
2. Bills added a hooked blade and a spike perpendicular to the pole to a spear-point tip.
3. Halberds replaced the bill's spike with an axe.
All were mounted on 6ft wooden shafts at sea, longer shafts being too unwieldy.

Arquebuses

4. Arquebuses were matchlock weapons. A slow match ignited the priming powder. Arquebuses reloaded slowly, but could be fired prior to boarding.

Crossbows

5. These ranged weapons were also used prior to boarding. They could be loaded more quickly than arquebuses, but typically had less penetrating power.

Swords

6. Swords were the most common weapon used at sea. Men wielding pole arms frequently carried a sword, as a reserve weapon.

Knives

7. Sailors routinely carried knives to carry out their duties aloft. These could double as weapons in time of need. Most soldiers carried a long knife along with their other weapons.

COMBAT

Individual duels between two galleons, especially naval vessels, were often written about, but rarely occurred. Galleons were intended to fight as part of a squadron. A lone galleon, sailing individually, would run when confronted by a dozen or more enemy galleons. For that matter, a squadron of galleons normally fled if confronted by a superior foe. There was no advantage to losing; a better opportunity might arise later.

A galleon cruising independently was generally looking for prizes, the more valuable the better. Merchant carracks were its prey, not well-defended enemy galleons. Winning a battle against an enemy galleon brought a rich reward of glory, but little money (unless it was known to be carrying treasure). Beating an enemy warship might also inflict so much damage that the cruise would get cut short. For those cruising 'on account' (only collecting prize money), this meant foregoing potential prizes. Such encounters were best avoided.

Galleons operating in a fleet or escorting a convoy were constrained by their responsibilities. They could not chase after that lone enemy galleon that appeared over the horizon, lest they leave their convoy unprotected or depart the fleet without permission. A galleon duel was usually the exception.

However, exceptions do occur, as demonstrated by the three galleon duels examined here. They also offer us three different types of battle. When the *Golden Hind* encountered the *Nuestra Señora de la Concepción*, it was fighting a known warship of roughly equal power. The battle occurred because *Nuestra Señora* was known to hold treasure. It is also an example of a pure boarding action.

The battle between the *San Mateo* and several individual English galleons during the Battle of Gravelines illustrates a pure gunnery duel. It occurred only because the Spanish fleet was in disorder, and the English were motivated to pursue to protect England from invasion.

The last fight of the *Revenge* pitted a lone English galleon against a Spanish fleet, and demonstrates why individual galleons did not fight fleets. This exemplifies a mixed battle, one in which gunnery and boarding both played an important role.

A race-built English galleon under sail in the Channel. With its low forecastle and narrow, high sterncastle, it is characteristic of the English galleons that fought the Spanish Armada. (Author's collection)

GOLDEN HIND AND NUESTRA SEÑORA DE LA CONCEPCIÓN

On 1 March 1579, *Nuestra Señora de la Concepción* was moving slowly north from Callao, in what is now Peru, heading for Panama laden with silver and jewels. Around midday, its lookouts reported sighting a strange sail. The sighting raised no alarm. *Nuestra Señora* was in the Pacific, a Spanish lake. The sail was certainly Spanish, possibly a ship from Valparaíso south of Callao, also carrying cargo to Panama.

Nuestra Señora's captain, San Juan de Antón, would not have worried about the strange sail, as it could not be hostile. In 1579, only Spain knew how to cross the oceans from the southern tip of South America. The route was a closely guarded secret, one guarded by the ferocious weather in the region.

If the strange sail were hostile, *Nuestra Señora* was well defended: it had numerous guns (although none were heavy), and a contingent of soldiers. The ship was reputed

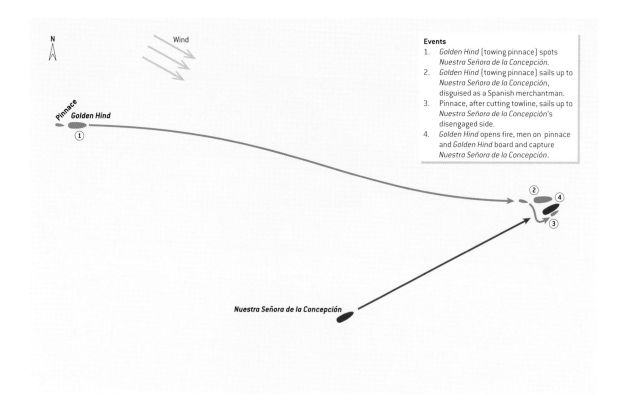

N

Wind

Events

1. *Golden Hind* (towing pinnace) spots
   Nuestra Señora de la Concepción.
2. *Golden Hind* (towing pinnace) sails up to
   Nuestra Señora de la Concepción,
   disguised as a Spanish merchantman.
3. Pinnace, after cutting towline, sails up to
   Nuestra Señora de la Concepción's
   disengaged side.
4. *Golden Hind* opens fire, men on pinnace
   and *Golden Hind* board and capture
   Nuestra Señora de la Concepción.

Pinnace
Golden Hind

①

② ④
③

Nuestra Señora de la Concepción

Drake's capture of *Nuestra Señora de la Concepción*.

to carry over 40 cannon and was nicknamed *Cacafuego* (usually translated as 'spit-fire', but literally meaning 'shit-fire'). It was a galleon, with a dedicated gun deck, but its tonnage was only 120 tons, and even a demi-culverin, firing a 9 lb shot, weighed 3,000 lb. Had it carried 40 heavy guns, it would have sacrificed half of its cargo-carrying capacity.

The main battery was probably made up of old and light bombards, most likely five or six on a side. To get the count near 40 required including the light man-killing guns throwing 1 lb and ½ lb shot, and even the swivels mounted in the tops. The crew probably did not exceed 100, and was probably fewer than this, perhaps 60. This would have comprised 40–60 mariners, and 20–40 officers and soldiers.

This was fewer soldiers than Spanish ships typically carried, but *Nuestra Señora* was in the Pacific. On the Atlantic side, a Spanish ship had to face privateers from virtually every European nation, and needed a bigger marine contingent. On the Pacific, all that was needed was sufficient soldiers to defend against indigenous tribes armed with light weapons and usually unprotected bodies. Twenty arquebusiers were sufficient for such needs.

As the day wore on, the strange sail grew nearer, but appeared to be a merchantman, a sluggish sailer. While it had appeared on the horizon shortly after noon, it had taken most of the daylight hours to close the short distance to *Nuestra Señora*. Only as dusk arrived did the ship come close enough to hail *Nuestra Señora*.

The ship was not Spanish: it was *Golden Hind*, a small English galleon, 14 months out of Plymouth. Commanded by Francis Drake, it was the sole remaining ship of six that sailed from the Devon port on 17 December 1577 intent on sailing into the

Pacific through the Straits of Magellan. The others had sunk or turned back. Drake was blown nearly to Antarctica in doing so, but by 1 November 1578, he was in the Pacific.

From there, Drake sailed north, along South America's Pacific coast, sacking cities, raiding the coast whenever he saw a likely target and snapping up the small coastal merchant vessels carrying silver and jewels north. The latter ships were unarmed: carrying cannon reduced cargo capacity, and there had hitherto been no threat greater than indigenous peoples firing bows from balsa rafts. Nor were Spanish cities and settlements well garrisoned: often, Drake's crew outnumbered any defenders.

News travelled by the speed of a ship, and *Golden Hind* outpaced any messenger carrying warning. The first notice Spanish ships or garrison received of the presence of a threat was the sight of Drake's topsails. Even then, as with *Nuestra Señora*, the warning went unrecognized until Drake attacked.

On 7 February, Drake attacked and sacked Callao, the port for the Viceroyalty of Peru's capital Lima. Callao was a collection point for Spain's New World silver, and was such a rich prize that Drake needed a week to squeeze the city dry of treasure. He also learned of the *Nuestra Señora*, and the cargo it was carrying to Panama. On the morning of 14 February, *Golden Hind* set off in pursuit, towed out of Callao harbour by its longboat. A few hours later, the Viceroy of Peru, Don Francisco de Toledo, and 200 Spanish soldiers stormed into Callao, too late to catch their quarry.

Golden Hind was a small galleon, displacing 300 tons. It was possibly smaller than *Nuestra Señora*, but not appreciably so. It was better armed, carrying 22 guns. Exactly which guns it carried is unknown today, but it most likely bore 14 demi-culverins, with four falcons and four falconettes. It was unlikely to have carried a heavier broadside. Any gun heavier than a demi-culverin would have caused sufficient hull damage to prevent completion of the voyage. It began the voyage with 80 men aboard,

A map of Drake's circumnavigation of the world. Only the second circumnavigation of the globe, it created a sensation upon its completion. This map was created in 1581, and is believed to have been printed in Antwerp. (Library of Congress)

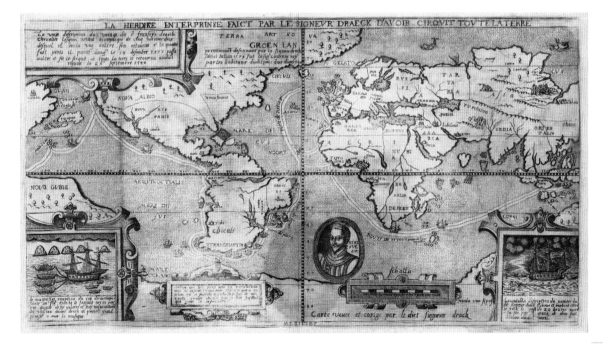

but by February 1579, the crew was closer to 60. There had been losses – to disease, the hazards of the sea and combat.

The chase lasted two weeks. Along the way, Drake captured another vessel that was laden with ship's cordage, a welcome discovery for a vessel that had gone without replacement rope since Plymouth. The capture also contained an emerald-studded gold crucifix. Emeralds from the confiscated cross may have been used in the new crown Elizabeth wore after the *Golden Hind*'s return.

The *Golden Hind* found *Nuestra Señora* at midday. Drake could have caught the Spanish ship by mid-afternoon with the press of sail *Golden Hind* had set, but Drake preferred to attack at dusk. He needed to slow *Golden Hind* without making it apparent the ship was slowing. Taking in sail could alert the Spanish something was amiss. Thus, Drake had several wine casks tied to lines and dragged them behind the ship. These slowed the ship without changing its course or sail plan.

While *Golden Hind* was still hull-down to its prey, its crew hastily altered its appearance to make it look like an unarmed merchantman. This probably consisted of closing the gunport lids, and covering over the upper gunports (which lacked lids) with canvas. They probably also removed any weathercloths with martial symbols, either by removing the strips of painted canvas covering the upper-deck railings, or by flipping them so the unpainted sides were exposed. The voyage around the cape had given the ship the careworn, weathered appearance typical of merchant craft.

The ruse worked. No one aboard *Nuestra Señora* suspected the approaching ship was an armed enemy boat. They allowed *Golden Hind* to sail alongside the Spanish ship's starboard, presuming it wanted to exchange news. It was only after the English ship began tossing grappling irons into *Nuestra Señora* to keep it from escaping that her captain, San Juan de Antón, realized something was wrong.

A Basque who had spent time in Southampton when England and Spain were allies, Antón spoke English fluently. Suddenly, men in the other ship began shouting: 'We're English. Strike sail. If not … we will send you to the bottom.' Antón replied defiantly, perhaps disbelieving an English ship was next to his, 'What England is this? Come on board and strike the sails yourselves.'

No further invitation was needed. A trumpet sounded. A volley of arquebus shot and crossbow bolts followed. *Golden Hind*'s guns fired a broadside, but not with ship-killing round shot: the guns were loaded with chain shot, intended to disable rigging. This broadside sheared *Nuestra Señora*'s mizzenmast.

At virtually the same time, a party of archers from *Golden Hind* swarmed aboard *Nuestra Señora*'s unengaged side. *Golden Hind* had sent its pinnace laden with men around both ships' sterns to the Spaniard's larboard side.

Faced with an unexpected two-front assault, Spanish resistance collapsed – or rather, it had no time to organize itself. The Spanish crew surrendered without firing a shot, and without suffering any casualties. Although the assault was full of sound and fury, it was a bloodless conquest.

Golden Hind spent the next three days transferring *Nuestra Señora*'s cargo to the English ship. The haul

A romanticized 1626 depiction of the fight between *Golden Hind* and *Nuestra Señora de la Concepción*. The print is wrong in several particulars: it shows the ships heading in opposite directions, while *Golden Hind* was actually sailing in the same direction, and the two galleons are incorrectly named. (Author's collection)

Caca Fogo.

Caca Plata.

was enormous, somewhere between half a million to one-third of a million pesos – worth over £22.5 million (or $30 million) today. Combined with its other plunder, it left *Golden Hind* almost full, unable to add more loot without endangering its seaworthiness.

After the transfer was complete, Drake released *Nuestra Señora* and its crew: he had no need of either of them, and it was simpler to release both. Before doing so, he showered the crew with gifts, comprising clothing, knives and a handful of money each – no doubt, from the silver pesos carried aboard *Nuestra Señora*. Captain Antón was more lavishly rewarded: Drake gave him a silver bowl inscribed with Drake's name, 600 lb of iron, a barrel of gunpowder and a German musket.

Generally, a good time was had by all. The English and Spanish departed happy, the captain had his ship restored and its crew had been enriched beyond their standard pay by Drake's generosity. The English had a ship filled with treasure. The only loser was the King of Spain.

SAN MATEO AT THE BATTLE OF GRAVELINES

As 29 July 1588 dawned, the Spanish galleon *San Mateo* was already having a bad day. The previous sunset had the ship anchored off Calais. One of ten galleons in the Squadron of Portugal, it was part of the Armada executing Philip II's Enterprise of England, which sought to replace Queen Elizabeth with a Catholic monarch.

San Mateo was in an elite squadron of what Britain now calls the Spanish Armada. Along with the Squadron of Castile, the Squadron of Portugal provided the invasion force's main combat strength. Eight of the squadron's galleons were built in Portugal, becoming part of Spain's fleet after Philip II assumed the Portuguese throne.

San Mateo was one of the intermediate-sized galleons in a squadron containing ships displacing 350–1,050 tons. One of the more powerful ships in the Armada, *San Mateo* was built in 1579 as *São Mateus* (Portuguese for St Matthew, the apostle). It displaced 750 tons, and carried 34 guns, which would all have been cast bronze muzzleloaders. When it left Spain, it carried a crew of 110, and 286 soldiers. Its captain, Don Diego Pimentel, was a courageous fighter.

The Armada's goal was to permit Spanish troops in the Netherlands under the command of the Duke of Parma to safely cross the English Channel to England. The Spanish Armada anchored off Calais, in anticipation of Parma's army departing for England, but the army was not ready. Alonso Pérez de Guzmán, Duke of Medina Sidonia, commanding the Armada, was told by Parma it would take a week or two to load his army on landing barges.

One disappointment had followed another since the Spanish arrival in the Channel on 19 July, and the Duke of Parma's news added more woe. A half-hearted attempt to seize Plymouth on 21 July was foiled by the English fleet arriving unexpectedly early. An effort to split the English fleet by isolating those in Plymouth from those in Southampton before destroying each in detail, misfired when the two parts merged, confounding the Spanish.

THE SILVER CHAIN

By the 1570s, much of Spain's silver and gems were coming from Pacific-coast territories, most notably silver from Potosí in the Viceroyalty of Peru. The problem was getting the treasure to Spain. It was too risky to send treasure ships through the Straits of Magellan. Instead, Pacific cargoes were shipped to Panama, on the Panama Isthmus's Pacific coast. From Panama, cargoes were carried overland by mule train to Nombre de Dios on the Caribbean Sea, and thence taken by ship to Havana, Cuba in the Gulf of Mexico.

Transporting the cargoes over the mountainous spine of the Panama Isthmus was safer than sailing a heavily laden ship through the Straits of Magellan.

Along with other treasure from Mexico, and the Spanish Main (South America's Gulf and Caribbean coast), these cargoes would then be loaded onto the annual treasure fleet to Spain. The fleet would stop at the Azores, before continuing to Seville. This route was well known to the British, who often sought out Spanish treasure ships along this route.

The Spanish Armada enters the English Channel. The ships in the foreground are galleons and galleasses. As long as the Spanish kept in a tight formation, the English found it difficult to attack individual ships. (Author's collection)

Two large Spanish ships were lost that day: *San Salvador* was damaged beyond repair when its powder magazine exploded; and *Nuestra Señora del Rosario* lost its bowsprit in a collision, fell behind and was captured that night by none other than Sir Francis Drake, aboard *Revenge*. Two days of frustrating and inconclusive skirmishing off the Isle of Portland followed.

On 25 July, an attempt to land on the Isle of Wight was as unsuccessful as the effort to take Plymouth. Hard fighting kept the English from carrying off two straggling ships.

San Mateo was in the thick of fighting between the 21st and the 25th. It assisted flagship *San Martín* in the rescue of the carrack *Gran Grin* on 21 July. While it did not fire a single cannon that day, by 25 July it was low on cannonballs and corned gunpowder. Five days of running battle consisted of the English (using their long-range culverins) firing at the Spanish at ranges too great for the Spanish guns to effectively return fire on the English ships. Fortunately for Spain, the ranges at which the English fired left shots that hit with insufficient energy to seriously damage hulls, although they did inflict damage on rigging, spars and personnel. The strain of being hit without replying was too great. The Spanish returned fire, expending irreplaceable cannon balls.

By 26 July, both sides were low on ammunition. Neither side fired their guns during the next two days, as the Armada drifted in light winds to Calais, where it anchored on 28 July. Calais, although a French port, was a good place to wait while Parma assembled his army in the Netherlands.

At Drake's urging, supported by Lord Howard of Effingham, commanding the English fleet, ten fireships were launched at the Spanish anchorage. In the first hours of 29 July, these ships, loaded with incendiaries, were set on fire. With sails set and tillers lashed to hold their courses, the burning vessels drifted down on the Spanish ships in the anchorage.

The Spanish panicked, believing they were not mere fireships, but explosive ships. Half the Armada cut their anchor cables; the rest weighed anchor. All, including *San Mateo*, fell to windward in disorder.

Morning found *San Mateo* doing its job: protecting the transports. It joined flagship *San Martín* and eight other galleons of the squadrons of Portugal and Castile between the Spanish carracks and the English.

At dawn, the English found the Armada scattered downwind of Calais. The English were low on cannonballs. Bombarding a foe until the ship received enough damage to sink or strike used cannonballs at a ferocious rate. The English had saved their few remaining cannonballs for a crisis or an opportunity, and the Spanish disarray was the opportunity the English sought: they swept in. The Battle of Gravelines followed, a wild mêlée, made up of scores of individual ship-to-ship duels.

If the English were low on powder and shot, so were the Spanish. The English ships received resupply from shore, and Howard had redistributed ammunition among his most effective ships. The Spanish only had the ammunition they brought from Spain, which averaged about 80 rounds per gun for the galleons. The galleons most heavily involved in combat, including *San Mateo*, had already used most of their ammunition, and were awaiting resupply from the Duke of Parma. Nor did Medina Sidonia redistribute his ammunition, as Howard had done.

That left *San Mateo* dangerously low on cannonballs when the battle opened, perhaps ten rounds per gun or even less – enough for an hour's combat. Even conserving ammunition, *San Mateo* would shoot itself out in two hours. Gravelines would last for eight hours.

The English galleons challenging *San Mateo* are unknown. They would have been with Drake's squadron, as he was in the lead during the pursuit. The first galleon to attack *San Mateo* was almost certainly one of the smaller, swifter ships, perhaps the 200-ton *Tiger*, armed with four culverins and eight demi-culverins, or the 100-ton

Charles Howard, Earl of Nottingham, Baron of Effingham, was England's Lord High Admiral from 1585 to 1619. He commanded the English fleet during the Armada campaign and the 1591 expedition to the Azores. (United States Navy Heritage and History Command)

65

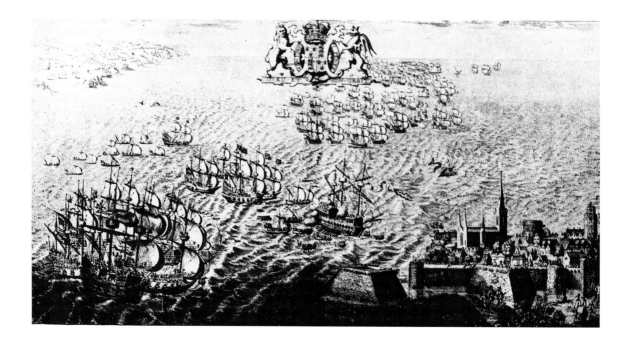

Fireships caused the Armada to scatter. With the Spanish in disorder, the English galleons used the opportunity to attack and destroy Spanish ships. (Author's collection)

Achates, which, despite its diminutive size, carried six demi-culverins. Whichever ship it was, it closed range to make every shot count.

Pimentel almost certainly ordered fire returned. The English ships were close enough to make shooting back worth it, but it had little effect on those ships. They fired a few quick broadsides, and then ranged ahead of *San Mateo* in pursuit of the Spanish carracks downwind. Other ships of Drake's squadron engaged the knot of Spanish galleons in passing, ranging close, but pressing on after a few broadsides to chase the rest of the Spanish fleet.

By the time the larger galleons caught up with *San Mateo*, its shot lockers were empty. As its fire slowed, the English ships drew closer – first engaging at 200 yards, then at arquebus range, and at the end 'one pike's length' from *San Mateo*. Even at 200–300 yards, a strike from a culverin would cause structural damage. Gunwale to gunwale, it would have gone through the ship.

Finally, one large English galleon closed with *San Mateo* and poured fire into the Spanish ship. The English ship is unknown, but it was a powerful one. Its broadsides reduced *San Mateo* to a sinking condition. It probably carried demi-cannon along with culverins, knocking enough holes in *San Mateo* so that the pumps could not keep up. Possibly, it was one of the new 500-ton race-built galleons constructed between 1586 and 1588. These included *Rainbow* and *Vanguard*. Alternatively, it could have been one of the ships rebuilt to Hawkins' specifications, such as *Elizabeth Bonaventure* or *Victory*. All were present, and all carried heavy batteries.

San Mateo was not defenceless. Its arquebusiers could still shoot, and poured down fire on the ships that closed. When one English sailor, excited by the success of the day, boarded *San Mateo* as his ship was firing into it, the Englishman was cut down.

That did not prevent *San Mateo* from being battered to a wreck. By the end of the battle, it had two divers working over the side to patch holes below the waterline with lead and tow. They begged a third diver from *San Martín*, which Medina Sidonia sent over. The water still rushed in faster than the pumps could drain it. *San Mateo* drifted astern, and then grounded near the mouth of the Scheldt. When three Dutch ships attacked it, Pimentel finally surrendered.

THE LAST FIGHT OF THE *REVENGE*

Following the Armada campaign, England launched almost annual expeditions to destroy Spanish warships at port in Spain, and to capture homebound Spanish treasure ships. Destroying Spanish warships was the English government's priority, whereas capturing Spanish treasure ships was the main concern of English admirals and captains. Thus, 1591 found an English fleet at Flores in the Azores, mid-Atlantic islands astride the return route of Spain's annual treasure fleet.

Two dozen English ships were anchored at Flores on 30 August, under the command of Thomas Howard, Earl of Suffolk. It included five 500-ton race-built galleons. Three – *Revenge*, *Elizabeth Bonaventure* and *Nonpareil* – were Armada campaign veterans, as was the slightly smaller 360-ton galleon *Foresight*. These were the largest ships in the English fleet (the rest were under 200 tons, with most displacing fewer than 120 tons), and served as gun platforms. The large galleons, including *Revenge*, carried crews of 250 men. The crews of the remaining ships were 60 men or less.

The English arrived in May, expecting the treasure fleet to arrive by July at the latest, but the treasure fleet was late that year. The delay allowed the governor of the Azores to send word to Spain. A fleet of 59 Spanish ships was dispatched to Terceira Island in the eastern Azores, home to the islands' main town Angra do Heroísmo. The fleet included 16 galleons and 18 large, armed carracks.

Five galleons were new, forming part of the Twelve Apostles built after the Armada campaign. These copied features of England's race-built ships, and were lower and significantly faster than Spanish galleons built prior to 1588. They were also significantly larger than the English galleons. *San Pablo* and *San Felipe* displaced 1,480 tons, *San Andrés* 1,060 tons, *San Bernabé* 875 tons and *Santo Tomás* 775 tons. They carried fewer guns than they were pierced for, due to Spanish artillery shortages. Yet all the Spanish warships carried at least 100 soldiers in addition to their crews. The largest galleons carried 320 soldiers. Without guns to take full advantage of their new designs, soldiers made up the deficit.

The English anchored at Ponte Delgada, on Flores Island's northern coast. The Spanish fleet arrived at Flores at dawn on 31 August, south of Flores. The Spanish commander, Alonso de Bazán, split the fleet. The larger portion went up the west side of Flores, downwind of any fleeing English ships. The smaller force, comprising seven galleons and four other warships, sailed up the east coast, upwind of the English. De Bazán planned to trap the English between the two parties.

The English learned of the approaching Spanish ships, weighed anchor and left port, initially assuming the ships to the west were the Spanish treasure fleet. Soon only *Revenge* remained.

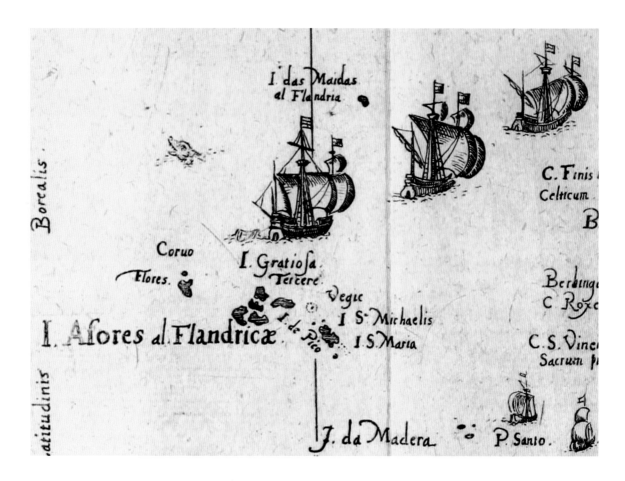

The map shows labels including: *Borealis*, *latitudinis*, *I. das Maidas al Flandria*, *Coruo*, *Flores*, *I. Gratiofa*, *Tercere*, *I. Aſores al Flandricæ*, *I. de Pico*, *Vegie*, *I S. Michaelis*, *I S. Maria*, *J. da Madera*, *P. Santo*, *C. Finis Celticum*, *B*, *Berlinga*, *C. Roxe*, *C. S. Vince Sacrum p*

No one knows why *Revenge* was tardy. The English later claimed that loading the sick aboard delayed her sailing. In argument against this, all the English ships had sick sailors, often as many as *Revenge*. It might have been that *Revenge*, the ship closest to shore, was becalmed, blanketed by mountains; or her captain, Richard Grenville, believed his ship was fast enough to catch the English fleet, and was taking extra care preparing for sea. Regardless, by the time the English finally spotted the western Spanish force and realized these were warships of Spain's Armada and not the treasure ships, the two sets of Spanish warships lay between *Revenge* and Howard's ships. Howard, recognizing his ships were outclassed by the larger and more heavily manned Spanish force, stood upwind of the Spanish, where they could not catch him.

Revenge's position was not hopeless. The eastern contingent of the Spanish fleet was already north of Ponte Delgada, pursuing the English main body. Grenville could have run west between the coast and the Spanish rear, sailing south to escape the Spanish. Grenville avoided this safe course, for it might separate him from the main body. He ordered *Revenge* cleared for action, and chose to sail after Howard, in the gap between the two Spanish forces. He gambled that he could sail through the gap before the Spanish closed it.

Three years earlier, Grenville would have won this bet. The Armada campaign showed galleons like *Revenge* could outsail any Spanish galleon. Grenville's calculations were based on outdated experience: the new generation of Spanish galleons built since 1588 were faster than their predecessors. Grenville would have to sail through the Spanish line.

Boldly approaching the Spanish, Grenville fired a broadside into the nearest galleons, forcing them to luff, opening a gap in the line. *Revenge* slipped through the gap in the windward squadron of Spanish galleons. The Spanish set off in pursuit. The older Spanish galleons, including *San Martín*, the 1588 Armada's flagship, fell behind. The new galleons, *San Felipe* and *San Bernabé*, did not. *San Felipe*, the largest Apostle and three times the size of *Revenge*, gained on *Revenge*, getting upwind of her.

San Felipe was pierced for 66 guns, but only had 37 aboard. The largest guns she had were two stone-throwing pedreros – short-barrelled, short-range, brass breechloaders. *San Felipe* had 223 soldiers aboard that day, all of whom were picked volunteers.

By contrast, *Revenge* carried 42 guns on 31 August; two demi-cannon (30 lb shot), four cannon-perriers (24 lb), ten culverins, eight demi-culverins, ten sakers and eight smaller guns. While it had 250 men aboard, 90 were sick and unable to fight. They were placed below the waterline, on the ballast.

Having gotten upwind, *San Felipe* closed on *Revenge*, intent on boarding. When the ships drew close, *San Felipe*'s captain, Don Claudio de Beamonte, ordered his trumpeter to sound a challenge, and saluted Grenville with his sword. Grenville returned the salute, and ordered a broadside fired into the Spanish galleon.

As the two ships touched, the Spanish threw grappling irons across to *Revenge*, intending to lash the ships together. *Revenge* fired a full broadside into *San Felipe* – the lower battery into the hull, the upper battery raking the decks – to clear it of boarders.

It was a shattering blow. *San Felipe* received critical hull damage. Of the six grappling lines thrown to *Revenge*, only one held. It parted. Only ten boarders managed to jump to *Revenge* before the two ships drifted apart. *San Felipe* fell to windward, crippled.

But *San Felipe* stopped *Revenge*. The Spanish galleon was so much larger than *Revenge* its sails blanketed the English galleon. By the time *Revenge*'s sails were drawing again, she had come to a standstill.

After *Revenge* became entangled with *San Bernabé*, the fight devolved into an 18-hour boarding battle. *San Bernabé* was eventually joined by four other Spanish ships, causing *Revenge* to fight five (not 15, as reported by Sir Walter Raleigh) Spanish vessels simultaneously. *Revenge* sank two of these. (Author's collection)

Neptuni proles, qui magni Martis alumnus
GRENVILVS patrias sanguine tinxit aquas

Richard Grenville commanded *Revenge* in its last fight. While an experienced mariner, explorer and fighting captain, he fatally underestimated Spanish capabilities. (Author's collection)

Before it could gain way, a second galleon, *San Bernabé*, caught up with *Revenge*. *Revenge* poured broadsides into *San Bernabé*, again causing great damage. Despite this, *San Bernabé* successfully lashed itself to *Revenge*. Entangled, the two ships' crews fought each other, with *San Bernabé* sending waves of boarders onto *Revenge*, whose crew drove them off.

Night had now fallen. Howard would not send his outnumbered ships to rescue *Revenge*. Supply ship *George Noble*, within hailing distance when the action started, asked what assistance Grenville required. Grenville told the ship to save itself.

The fight between *Revenge* and *San Bernabé* was even odds, but the odds changed when other Spanish ships joined in. The 26-gun, 700-ton *San Cristóbal* came up after dark, ramming *Revenge* in the stern; although *San Cristóbal*'s bow was damaged, her soldiers soon boarded *Revenge*. Although its attacks were not coordinated with those of *San Bernabé*, it still forced *Revenge* to split between the two parties. The old, 530-ton galleon *Asunción* joined the fight next, tying itself to *Revenge*'s bow, just ahead of *San Bernabé*. The flyboat *La Serena* joined *Asunción* at the bow, ramming *Asunción* in the dark in its haste to join the fray.

Beset by four ships, *Revenge* fought throughout the night, taking casualties, including Grenville. But its men fought on, repelling all boarding attempts, sinking *Asunción* with her bow chasers, and damaging *La Serena* so badly that she sank shortly after daybreak.

Dawn saw *Revenge* with 150 dead. Most of the rest were wounded. *Revenge* was dismasted during the night; her upperworks were ruined. The Spanish lost hundreds dead, and had two ships sunk and three galleons seriously damaged. Grenville, badly wounded, refused to surrender, ordering the gunner to light *Revenge*'s magazine, rather than giving her to the Spanish. His subordinates ignored his order. *Revenge*'s master boarded Don Alonso's flagship, asking for terms. Don Alonso offered *Revenge*'s crew generous terms to end the fight: her survivors would be spared and repatriated to England. The English accepted, and Don Alonso honoured the terms.

Grenville died of wounds aboard the Spanish flagship, *San Pablo*. *Revenge*, along with several Spanish ships, sank in a storm, probably a hurricane, which swept through the Azores in September. Its English survivors were returned to England that autumn. An epic legend arose in the wake of the battle: the last fight of the *Revenge*.

ANALYSIS

The highlighted battles show how England and Spain pursued different strategies and tactics. Both England and Spain cut their coats to fit the cloth they had available. In the case of England, manpower, especially soldiers, was always an issue. England had no standing army and depended on trained bands – men picked by their communities to train two days a month – and untrained militia. The crown lacked the funds to maintain a large navy. Throughout the century, the Royal Navy never had more than 20 warships. Rarely were more than six in active commission at the same time.

Yet England had plenty of mariners, and was Europe's artillery founding centre in the 16th century. It also had people willing and able to fund privateering expeditions and build warships in joint-stock ventures. (It helped that most ordinary merchant vessels had to be armed due to piracy.) In emergencies, the crown could call on these vessels as a reserve.

One result was that English galleons were small. Of the 34 'Queen's ships' in the English fleet during the Armada campaign, only five were larger than 600 tons. None of the eight Queen's ships sent out in 1591 to the Azores were greater than 600 tons. The largest ships the Royal Navy could afford to build displaced between 500 and 1,000 tons.

The private ships (armed merchantmen run by their owners under royal colours) were even smaller. The largest ran at 300 tons, and two-thirds were 100 tons or less. Private builders preferred smaller ships: three ships of 150 tons were preferred to one ship of 450 tons, as three ships tripled the opportunities to find prizes, while reducing the risk of losing one's entire investment compared to if a single ship were lost.

There were other advantages to smaller ships. They were generally faster, mostly because they had lower superstructures, an advantage accentuated by the English race-built design, which had a minimal forecastle and sterncastle. By the end of the era, the

ARCA RALE
Admiral

Ark Royal was one of the larger Royal ships at 800 tons. It was built as a private venture, but purchased by the crown prior to the Armada campaign, where it served as the English flagship. Note the longboat towed astern. (United States Navy Heritage and History Command)

quarter-deck comprised only a single level, and the forecastle was being replaced by the half-deck, quarter-deck and poop. This design dominated the remaining 250 years of fighting sail.

Smaller size did not make the English ships weaker. They had sturdy hulls, and more importantly, they mounted unprecedentedly heavy artillery batteries. The 20 guns on *Revenge*'s lower gun deck were capable of throwing a broadside of 186 lb of iron shot. Its upper deck could throw another 50 lb. This was typical of the larger English galleons. *Elizabeth Bonaventure* carried two cannon, two demi-cannon, 11 culverins and 12 demi-culverins – a broadside of 350 lb. The 500-ton *Vanguard* had a broadside of 250 lb, while during the Armada campaign, *Nonpareil* could fire 187 lb.

These were ship-killing large guns. *Revenge* knocked *San Felipe* out of the battle with two close-range broadsides. *San Felipe* was three times the tonnage of *Revenge* and just out of the shipyard. Similarly, *San Mateo* and an earlier *San Felipe* suffered similar fates during the Armada campaign. Both ships were so badly battered by English galleons at the Battle of Gravelines as to be reduced to a sinking state, and were subsequently abandoned.

Spain similarly built ships to match its capabilities, and its past experiences. Spain was rich through New World treasure and (after it had absorbed Portugal) East Indies spices. Yet its mercantile and manufacturing classes were miniscule, and the crown rigidly controlled commerce and manufacturing. Spain had a significant merchant marine, and those ships could and were conscripted for naval service when needed, but these were secondary to the crown's warships.

Because of its weak manufacturing sector, Spain's metalworking industry was small, largely limited to crown-controlled foundries. It lacked the ability to turn out large numbers of heavy cannon. The cannon it did produce were inferior to English artillery in both quality and design. Spanish guns failed more frequently. Designs like the pedrero were within the capabilities of Spanish gunfounders, but inferior in performance to culverins, especially the long-barrelled, ship-killing versions cast in England. Spain failed to realize the potential of naval artillery until the Armada campaign. The Spanish treated naval warfare as a continuation of land warfare at sea. Ships were fortifications and bastions, and were to be taken by storm – using soldiers.

A Spanish galleon of the Armada period. Spanish galleons, built to crown orders rather than as commercial speculation, were larger and usually taller than their English counterparts. They were effective warships when battles were fought on Spanish terms. (United States Navy Heritage and History Command)

Until 1588, Spain built large galleons to serve as seagoing forts. The castles, stern and fore, were higher than those of other nations, sacrificing seaworthiness for combat ability. They gave the Spanish a military advantage offensively and defensively in boarding actions. Yet the lack of manoeuvrability, and their limited ability to sail into the wind, made it difficult to force a boarding action against the nimble English galleons.

The Spanish were not stupid. Once the limitation of their existing design was revealed during the Enterprise of England, Spain redesigned its ships to improve their seakeeping and manoeuvrability. The Twelve Apostles demonstrated Spain could build large ships capable of catching English warships, as exemplified during the Battle of Flores, when *San Felipe* caught *Revenge*.

A fortunate combination of wind, sea state and initial position helped. *San Felipe* was at its best point of sailing, while *Revenge* was committed to a course that moved it more slowly. *Revenge* was constrained by other Spanish ships from fleeing at its best point of sailing.

Yet even with better ships after 1588, Spain was still committed to boarding actions. It could not manufacture enough guns, much less heavy artillery, to fully arm its warships. Although it attempted to make up the difference by purchasing guns abroad (including from England), it failed to find enough guns to fully arm the five 'Twelve Apostles' ships accompanying Don Alonso in his 1591 Azores expedition. *San Pablo*, *San Bernabé*, *San Andrés* and *Santo Tomás* carried 42, 24, 25 and 25 guns respectively, but none were as large as a minion. The only heavy guns mounted by *San Felipe* were two pedreros. Of the 19 ships in the fleet carrying heavy guns, none carried more than five guns the size of a culverin or larger.

Spanish shortages in artillery led them to retain bombards longer than the English did. During the Armada campaign, up to three-quarters of the guns mounted in Spanish ships were iron breechloaders. (Author's collection)

The result was that battles between Spanish and English galleons ended up rather like a game where the side that forced its strategy on the opponent won the round. If the Spanish could force a boarding battle, the Spanish won. If the English could force an artillery duel, the English won. The few exceptions, where the English tried a boarding action and won (such as the duel between *Golden Hind* and *Nuestra Señora de la Concepción*), succeeded because they were ambushes. In the case of *Golden Hind*, surprise was total, and the Spanish never got an opportunity to resist.

A verso. These swivel-mounted guns were also known as falconets, serpentines and rabinets. They were breechloading, and generally built from iron. Although they were effective against personnel, they did not seriously damage a ship's hull or structure. (William Lardas)

Yet there was a contradiction within this dichotomy. The English could win battles, but at the cost of foregoing the taking of a ship as a prize. The Spanish could win battles, but only at the cost of high casualties. Neither side desired those outcomes.

Because England's exchequer was perpetually strapped, the English, even the Royal Navy, was in it for the money. It was not enough to simply win, to send enemy ships to the bottom: every expedition was expected to bring home a profit, either in ships and cargoes sold for prize money, or better still (as Drake did in 1579), with Spanish treasure in the holds of English ships.

Even during the Armada campaign, with the fate of England in the balance, English ships went haring off after prizes instead of battering the Spanish Armada. Drake did on the night of 22/23 July, when, instead of leading the English fleet against the Spanish, he doused his sternlights to chase and capture *Nuestra Señora del Rosario*. At Gravelines, Howard did the same, abandoning the chase of the fleeing Spanish to attempt a capture of *San Lorenzo*, a galleass that had already run aground.

One result was that English galleons rarely sought out battles with Spanish galleons. They preferred hunting easily captured carracks (which often surrendered, saving expense in gunpowder, repairs and blood). On the few occasions where they did attack galleons, they often fired at too great a range. This was illustrated by the first week's fighting during the Armada campaign, where they exhausted their ammunition without seriously damaging their foe. When they finally did close at Gravelines, they devastated their opponents.

Similarly, Spain found it difficult to force boarding actions. Those occurred only when an English galleon miscalculated, as at Flores, forcing the English galleon into action. Even when that did happen, the results were bloody, for both sides.

The bulwarks of the ships of the day were generally sturdy enough to resist arquebus or crossbow fire. While murdering pieces, as the small man-killing swivels and versos were termed, could penetrate superstructure bulwarks, these were relatively few and slow-firing. Capturing a ship meant putting men armed with cold steel aboard the enemy vessel.

That favoured the defender. Attacking boarders had to expose themselves to board the enemy ship, allowing the defenders (under partial cover) to pick them off. Once aboard, attackers were on unfamiliar territory, known intimately to the defenders, who could ambush the assailants.

The result was a lopsided casualty bill. The English defenders eventually lost, but at an excessive cost to the Spanish attackers. At Flores, *Revenge*'s crew lost 150 dead, and nearly 80 per cent of the survivors were injured. The Spanish lost almost three times that number killed, and had two ships sunk as well. It was an unsustainable exchange rate.

AFTERMATH

The Anglo-Spanish War of 1585–1604 ended a year after Elizabeth's death in March 1603. Philip II had died five years before Elizabeth, in September 1598. By 1604, the Dutch had achieved de facto independence. The war had been a costly drag on Spain since Philip III had replaced his father. England and the Dutch were tired of war. Spain had earlier made peace with France, which had ended its civil wars. Spain's finances were overextended, despite the vast treasure pouring in from the New World. James I, Elizabeth's successor, wanted to end a war whose two principal advocates were dead.

The Treaty of London, signed on 28 August 1604, restored Spain and England to the status quo before the war. England remained Protestant, while Spain kept its New World colonies and recognized the Treaty of Tordesillas as a dead letter. When England established Jamestown in North America in 1605, Spain tolerated its presence. The peace treaty was unpopular in Britain (since James ruled both England and Scotland), especially the English parts of Britain, but the king's will went further than it would do a century later.

The war's end brought down the curtain on the age of the galleon. These vessels would continue to be built for a few years more, and some true galleons probably lasted until the middle of the 17th century. The galleon would continue to be used as a courtesy type for a long time. The term galleon became synonymous with a treasure ship, regardless of the type of ship carrying the treasure. The Manila galleon that George Anson captured in 1742 was really a two-decker, similar to the Indiamen Britain was building at the time, not a galleon.

New types of warships emerged, the ship-of-the-line, the two-decker and the sloop-of-war. All of these borrowed elements from the galleon, but were new designs. The built-up beakhead disappeared. The forecastle became a single raised deck, used more for handling the ground tackle and foremast's lines. The sterncastle became the half-deck, quarter-deck and (if present) the poop. They were no longer superstructures. The hull went up to these new decks, increasing structural integrity. The lower gun deck ran flush along the hull without the drop aft.

The galleon remained popular in memory in both Spain and England. Both sides won enough victories to cherish individual ships. *Golden Hind* was turned into a museum ship until it rotted away in 1650. No one thought to record its dimensions and lines during the 70 years it existed, and these remain unknown. Several replicas of the ship have been built in modern times, including a reconstruction built in 1973.

A full-size replica of a Spanish galleon was built in Spain in 2009. The ship, *El Galeón Andalucia*, can best be described as an approximation. Compromises were accepted to allow paying guests to sail aboard the ship. It was built as an operating vessel, and tours extensively. It follows the seas travelled by historical Spanish galleons: the Mediterranean, northern Europe, the Caribbean and Gulf Coast and the North American Atlantic coast. It is worth a visit to see this ship, if you are interested in the era.

El Galeón Andalucia is a modern replica of a 16th-century Spanish galleon. It contains anachronisms. The spars have footropes, the guns are apparently cast iron and mounted on 17th-century truck carriages and the decks are spaced to fit 21st-century adults. Regardless, it offers a glimpse of life on a 16th-century vessel.
(Library of Congress)

BIBLIOGRAPHY

The galleon era was a period of rapid transition in both naval architecture and armament. As a result, it attracts the attention of modern scholars. One of my first stops when writing a book such as this is the Alumni Theses and Dissertations page of the Institute for Nautical Archaeology at Texas A&M University (https://nautarch. tamu.edu/academic/alum.htm). In this case, it yielded several useful documents which I used. You do not need to be a scholar or researcher to use it, and I recommend it to anyone interested in maritime history.

I also found much useful information on Archive.org. It contains a fascinating collection of material in the public domain, including many early publications of the Naval Records Society and Hakluyt Society. As a teen, growing up in Ann Arbor, MI, I could find many of these books in the University of Michigan Library, but few had access to such an array of material. Now, thanks to sites like Archive.org, everyone does.

Books marked with an asterisk are available online.

Archibald, E. H. H., *The Wooden Fighting Ship in the Royal Navy AD 897–1860*, Arco Publishing, New York, NY, 1968

Bojakowski, Katie Michelle Custer, *Exploration and Empire: Iconographic Evidence of Iberian Ships of Discovery*, doctoral dissertation, Texas A&M University, College Station, TX, 2011*

Corbett, Julian S., *Drake and the Tudor Navy, with a History of the Rise of England as a Maritime Power: In Two Volumes*, Longmans, Green, and Co., London, 1898*

Drake, Sir Francis, *The World Encompassed: Being his Next Voyage to that to Nombre de Dios*, The Hakluyt Society, London, 1855*

Earle, Peter, *The Last Fight of the Revenge*, Methuen Publishing, London, 1992

Friel, Ian, *The Good Ship: Ships, Shipbuilding and Technology in England 1200–1520*, Johns Hopkins University Press, Baltimore, MD, 1995

Hoskins, Sara Grace, *16th Century Cast-Bronze Ordnance at the Museu De Angra Do Heroísmo*, master's thesis, Texas A&M University, College Station, TX, 2003*

Howard, Frank, *Sailing Ships of War 1400–1860*, Mayflower Press, New York, NY, 1979

Kemp, Peter, *The Campaign of the Spanish Armada*, Facts on File, Inc. New York, NY, 1988

Kirsh, Peter, *The Galleon: The Great Ships of the Armada Era*, Conway Maritime Press, London, 1990

Laanela, Erika Elizabeth, *Instrucción Náutica (1587) By Diego García De Palacio: An Early Nautical Handbook from Mexico*, master's thesis, Texas A&M University, College Station, TX, 2008*

Lavery, Brian, *Anatomy of the Ship: The Colonial Merchantman Susan Constant, 1605*, Conway Maritime Press, London, 1988

Markham, Clements R., *Narratives of the Voyages of Pedro Sarmiento De Gamboa to the Straits of Magellan*, The Hakluyt Society, London, 1895*

McElogue, Douglas, *Anatomy of the Ship: Tudor Warship Mary Rose*, Naval Institute Press, Annapolis, MD, 2015

Nuttall, Zelia, *New Light on Drake: A Collection of Documents Relating to His Voyage of Circumnavigation, 1577–1580*, The Hakluyt Society, London, 1914*

Smith, Roger C., *Vanguard of Empire: Ships of Exploration in the Age of Columbus*, Oxford University Press, New York, NY, 1993

Valenti, Vincent Nicholas, *Transitions in Medieval Mediterranean Shipbuilding: A Reconstruction of the Nave Quadra of the Michael of Rhodes Manuscript*, master's thesis, Texas A&M University, College Station, TX, 2009*

One of the medals cast in England following the Spanish Armada to celebrate its defeat. This piece shows a Spanish ship breaking up, presumably a result of running aground on a rocky shore. (Library of Congress)

INDEX